Black Veterans, Politics, and Civil Rights in Twentieth-Century America

War and Society in Modern American History

Series Editor: Gregory A. Daddis

War has long been an integral part of United States history, shaping our national identity, conferring upon us our independence, settling the question of slavery in a divided nation, and propelling us to leadership on the world stage. Yet war equally has left an indelible impact in less positive ways, commanding substantial portions of our national budget, often dominating our approach to foreign policy, and disrupting societies abroad in devastating ways. This series aims to move beyond traditional military history focusing on commanders, campaigns, and battles. Rather, the works within the *War and Society in Modern American History* series aspire to evaluate how our society has gone to war, experienced war, and, perhaps most importantly, grappled with the social consequences of war. We therefore welcome original proposals and manuscripts on a wide array of themes—cultural, gender, religious, intellectual, and environmental to name but a few—that explore the connections between the human phenomenon of war and American society in the modern era.

Titles in the Series

Black Veterans, Politics, and Civil Rights in Twentieth-Century America: Closing Ranks, by Robert F. Jefferson Jr.

Black Veterans, Politics, and Civil Rights in Twentieth-Century America

Closing Ranks

Edited by Robert F. Jefferson Jr.

LEXINGTON BOOKS
Lanham • Boulder • New York • London

Published by Lexington Books
An imprint of The Rowman & Littlefield Publishing Group, Inc.
4501 Forbes Boulevard, Suite 200, Lanham, Maryland 20706
www.rowman.com

6 Tinworth Street, London SE11 5AL, United Kingdom

Copyright © 2019 by The Rowman & Littlefield Publishing Group, Inc.

All rights reserved. No part of this book may be reproduced in any form or by any electronic or mechanical means, including information storage and retrieval systems, without written permission from the publisher, except by a reviewer who may quote passages in a review.

British Library Cataloguing in Publication Information Available

Library of Congress Cataloging-in-Publication Data

Names: Jefferson, Robert F., 1963- editor.
Title: Black veterans, politics, and civil rights in twentieth-century America : closing ranks / edited by Robert F. Jefferson Jr.
Description: Lanham, MD : Lexington Books, [2019] | Series: War and society in modern American history | Includes bibliographical references and index.
Identifiers: LCCN 2018052112 (print) | LCCN 2018055013 (ebook) | ISBN 9781498586320 (Electronic) | ISBN 9781498586313 (cloth)
Subjects: LCSH: African American veterans--History--20th century. | African American veterans--Political activity. | African American veterans--Social conditions--20th century. | Civil rights movements--United States--History--20th century. | African American soldiers x History--20th century.
Classification: LCC UB357 (ebook) | LCC UB357 .B53 2019 (print) | DDC 323.196/073008697--dc23
LC record available at https://lccn.loc.gov/2018052112

Table of Contents

Foreword: "Looking Back and Looking Ahead"   ix
Hal M. Friedman

Acknowledgments   xiii

Introduction: Recovering the Scions of Jericho: America's Wars, Black Veterans Politics and Civil Rights in Twentieth-Century American History   xv
Robert F. Jefferson Jr.

1   "We Never Get to be Men": Big Bill Broonzy, Black Consciousness, and WWI's Returning Black Veterans   1
Kevin D. Greene

2   Frames Refocused: Blinded Black and White Ex-GIs and the Social Re-Orientation of Self in World War Two America   21
Robert F. Jefferson Jr.

3   Have Gun, Will Travel: The Deacons for Defense and Justice, Armed Self Defense and the Long Black Power Movement   41
Selika M. Ducksworth-Lawton

4   "The Military No More: Vietnam, Civil Rights, and Attitudes toward Change"   63
Jeremy P. Maxwell

5   African American Leadership's Tug of War with Black Military Service Members: Rhetorical Situation Strategies in the Face of Gulf War   81
Elizabeth F. Desnoyers-Colas

Afterword: How to Place These Fine Essays into Larger Contexts *Peter Karsten*	105
Selected Bibliography	113
Index	119
About the Contributors	123

Foreword

"Looking Back and Looking Ahead"

Hal M. Friedman

The intersection of war, society, military service, and civil rights politics has been written about significantly in the last few decades, as Robert Jefferson has illustrated in the introduction to this collection of essays. However, what has not been written about significantly is the postwar activism by veterans, and especially black veterans, when it comes to political activity meant to further civil rights agendas based on military service to the Republic. Historiographically, then, this collection of essays is a continuation of work begun several decades ago by Rayford Logan and continued by scholars such as John Shy, Peter Karsten, and Stephen Ortiz. Even more so, this collection is a beginning attempt to put that previous work into historical context and perspective at the beginning of the twenty-first century.

How the intersection of military service, civil rights activism, and concepts of patriotism have taken place is another area where these essays either continue the work of previous historians or break new ground. As Jefferson and his authors have shown, there is significant work that has been done on African American service in World War Two and its extraordinarily fundamental importance for the civil rights movement. However, civil rights struggles took place long before the 1940s and they have continued afterward. In fact, I would argue that this context is vitally important now since the American military enjoys such a high social status from the American public, including the African American community, but also continues to place civil rights obstacles in front of some of those very constituents.

Moreover, as both Jefferson and Selika Ducksworth-Lawton have illustrated, this history allows us to begin questioning "scripted" and conventional histories of the civil rights movement. We hardly hear, for example, about truly racially integrated situations such as Jefferson documented with the both black and white blind veterans in postwar New England. Even more at the core of matters, Ducksworth-Lawton's exploration of the Deacons brings into question just how successful "militant pacifism" was in the greater history of the civil rights movement. In fact, their essays in particular makes us question whether or not there were several civil rights movements, a hidden, a violent, or at least armed defensive one that almost no one knows about, and the nonviolent one that has become part of our conventional and even mythological history. Are there other civil rights movements or aspects to it that we just have not heard about?

Going back before the obviously key time periods of the 1940s, 1950s, and 1960s, what was the pre-1940 context of the civil rights movement? One of the deans of African American History, Darlene Clark Hine, argues that black professionals in the 1920s were the key and even the start of the modern civil rights movement. Kevin D. Greene illustrates that it again may have also been military service in World War One and amongst working-class blacks like Big Bill. Even more so, civil rights consciousness may easily have begun long before military service. As oppressive as the Jim Crow military was, Greene's essay allows us to ask the question of whether or not the Jim Crow military was still more an environment of freedom or at least less oppressive than civilian life (especially in the South) and if it was the military that was key to awakening civil rights consciousness because of the training, travel, pay, or combat experience? Skills such as organization, leadership, and communication that built confidence seem to be vital here as well, as they were later with groups like the Deacons.

Jefferson's work is central not only because of the unique situation in Connecticut that he describes but because no historian, to this author's knowledge, has looked at blind veterans' conditions after the war, probably because of their small number. Blindness raises a fascinating question, however, about civil rights consciousness. Did it take physical blindness, at least in this case, to overcome racist consciousness? Similarly, did it take "aggressive normalization" on the part of the people running the training facility? Here again, are there other dimensions of the civil rights movement that have been ignored or just not explored yet?

Ducksworth-Lawton's work on the Deacons is perhaps even more fundamental in getting us to question our assumptions about the civil rights movement. Do the Deacons represent a conservative (as defined before the rise of the Right in the 1970s) civil rights movement in contrast to the more liberal or left nonviolent wing of the movement? What exactly is the fascinating history of this group arguing and employing Second Amendment rights given the controversial nature of the gun lobby and gun rights in post-Vietnam America? What role does violence and nonviolence play in concepts of masculinity? Were the Deacons an example of a type of "offensive-defensive" counterinsurgency?

With the Vietnam War and after, the historiography gets thinner again given the focus on World War Two, and especially about postwar activity by black veterans. Jeremy Maxwell, however, has raised further important questions about black military service and civil rights activism during the war. Following on work by historians such as John Sherwood, Maxwell has us look heavily at class as an aspect of the civil rights movement, as did Greene, since there appear to be different civil rights movements again based on the African American community's leadership: older, more middle-class African Americans who may have been pre-1968 military veterans as opposed to younger, more working-class, militant, and drafted veterans between 1968 and 1973. Was it not just time period that dictated a more militant attitude while still in the service, but also social class, age, skills (or lack thereof), national political environment, and military status?

Elizabeth Desnoyers-Colas's work on the Persian Gulf War, while focused more on the war itself rather than the postwar period, also brings up important questions, not only about that conflict but the post–Cold War period and the Global War on Terrorism (GWOT). Again, like with Maxwell's essay, what role did social class play during the Persian Gulf War when her sources illustrate that it was primarily the African American leadership that so heavily questioned the war and central black participation in combat roles? What can historians in the future do to build on this work by getting at sources not only from the veterans themselves after the conflict, but from working-class African Americans during the war, especially since military service seems to have had such a positive status in the general African American community by the 1980s and after. Perhaps just as importantly, how did civil rights protests from leaders during the war impact veterans after the war and how did these political dimensions impact civil rights struggles among black service personnel and veterans during the Global War on Terrorism? Did the fact that there were senior black military leaders by this time, such as General Colin Powell, have any impact? How did the war galvanize civil rights struggles for other groups, most notably over sexual identity rights? A fascinating future study, for instance, would be the Persian Gulf War's impact on black gay and lesbian veterans in the 1990s and beyond.

If this foreword has raised more questions than it has answered, it is a tribute to Robert Jefferson and his authors for broaching so many new areas and looking again at so many older ones. There are clearly many dimensions of the civil rights movement that have not yet been explored or as explored as they need to be. There are even more clearly dimensions of the history of the civil rights movement's intersection with American military history that have barely been looked at. These essays are a good start and will hopefully lead to other historians taking up the challenge of documenting this intersection of American war and society.

Acknowledgments

Even before the first words met the light of day, this collection benefited from a group of true believers and interested converts. First, a great deal of credit goes to the talented group of authors in the volume. Such an endeavor has very little hope of getting off the ground without such a dedicated band of colleagues and scholars in the field of study. Each contributor spent hours poring over sections, passages, and research issues that were read and re-read perhaps way too often by reviewers both far and wide. To a person, they brought their expertise to bear on questions of race, civil rights, and war in ways that enriched the process for all concerned. One is truly blessed to have such an august community of first-rate professionals in his midst.

Special thanks also goes to scholars who attended the panel sessions of the 2015 annual meetings of the Organization of American Historians and the Society for Military History, where many of the ideas that shaped the creation of this collection first appeared. The insightful critiques and discussions along the way have informed much of the thinking that went into the configuration of the volume. Hopefully, the scholars, artists, and pundits who participated in these sessions will recognize their fingerprints in the form of the questions they raised about race, war, and civil rights among the pages in this collection.

I wish to also thank my editors Brian Hill and Eric Kuntzman for their enthusiastic interest in the volume. Their hands-on approach and unending font of support given throughout the process gave me a greater appreciation for the value of true intellectual camaraderie. Good fortune comes in all shapes and forms when it comes to navigating the world of academic publishing and one is indeed lucky when she or he meets a group of editors who are dedicated to the craft as they are.

Finally, I wish to express my unending gratitude to Lisa—my life partner, best friend, and personal muse for her untiring love, support, and much needed therapy throughout this project. While I worked on this collection, she managed to treat the dirty dishes, the unattended laundry, and the unanswered texts with the same aplomb as our bimonthly excursions to the Hot Springs of Truth or Consequences, New Mexico. With much love and affection, I dedicate this work to you!

Introduction

Recovering the Scions of Jericho: America's Wars, Black Veterans Politics and Civil Rights in Twentieth-Century American History

Robert F. Jefferson Jr.

For him, the story possessed many unexpected twists and turns, but it always seemed to end with a common refrain. In 1969, Rayford Whittingham Logan, a prominent African American historian at Howard University, provided incisive commentary on the significance of African American participation in America's wars and how it framed the struggles for equality waged by black veterans returning home from the fields of fire. Nearly thirty years earlier, he and fourteen other African American leaders submitted a collection of essays to the University of North Carolina (UNC) Press that expressed their aspirations for a world free from racial oppression and class antagonism. To them, the upheavals resulting from world war and the U.S. entry into the conflict permitted them to make such claims on American society.

However, their hopes proved apocryphal. After expressing grave reservations over the unanimous calls for end of racial discrimination, the UNC Press initially rejected the manuscript submitted by the famous black scholar and his contemporaries. After facing the prospect of intense legal action and an avalanche of negative public opinion, the reviewers reluctantly relented and the press published *What the Negro Wants*, a sterling compendium of essays that served as a useful preamble for the modern civil rights movement. But the battle over the authorship of the manuscript and the meaning surrounding the jarring calls for equality that appeared throughout its pages was not lost to the editor of the collection. Comparing the controversy surrounding the publication of the book to the long-distance gauntlet of war and race that blacks in uniform were forced to run abroad and at home during the course of the twentieth century, Logan opined:

The difficulty about publication was, I believe then and more so now, the demand for equal opportunity in the fulfillment of obligations as American citizens. Even in 1944, when Negroes on many battlefields were giving "the last full measure of devotion," the myth of the Negro's avoidance of his responsibilities persisted. Despite similar evidence of this "last full measure" in the Korean War and the war in Vietnam, even some "friendly" writers continue to condemn Negroes for insisting upon equality of opportunity without allegedly accepting equality of responsibility.[1]

In many ways, Logan's military experiences in the World War and his postwar political activities prefigured his remarks. Born in Washington, D.C., in 1897, he attended the prestigious M Street High School before going on to enter Williams College. There, Logan pursued a bachelors' degree in history and he had no sooner graduated in 1917 when fate in the form of war intervened. Eager to strike a blow for democracy and racial progress, he promptly translated these sentiments into action. He later recalled, "carried away by my own eloquence, I enlisted on July 10, 1917, as a buck private in the First Separate Battalion of District of Columbia National Guards." After receiving a promotion to first lieutenant, he was assigned to the all-black 92nd Infantry Division of the American Expeditionary Force and shipped to France in 1918.

But as he soon learned, the promises of American democracy didn't include the Williams College graduate and his fellow black cadre of the 372nd. Once they arrived in Saint Nazaire, the regimental commanding officer assigned Logan and other black officers to the smallest staterooms and ordered them to eat lunch with black stevedores. The bitter memories of American racial bigotry while facing the horrors of war greatly affected the future historian well into the decades of the 1930s and 1940s. So much so that when he and other black World War One veterans were invited to Washington, D.C., to appear before Congress during its discussions about the African American presence in the Selective Service, they didn't hesitate to recount their disillusioning experiences in the previous war in graphic detail.[2]

Rayford Logan's experience during the First World War and his postwar struggles against Jim Crow stand in the doorway of two overarching historical themes in the American experience. First, the interrelationships between war, politics, and society as demonstrated in the social experiences of former servicemen like Rayford Logan foreshadowed the social dimensions of the new military history for nearly four decades. Beginning in 1980, scholars like Peter Karsten, John Shy, Richard Kohn, Edward Coffman, and John Whiteclay Chambers had established a connection between war and military service and social, political, and economic structures. Exploring topics ranging from the American Revolutionary War, the Civil War, and World Wars One and Two, this cadre of historians asked critical questions about war's effect on society and what was the place of military service within the broader context of American life.[3] This generation of scholarship was soon followed by a community of scholars such as Wayne Lee, Mark Grimsley, and Elizabeth Fenn, who focused on linkages between culture, ideology, and military behavior. With their invaluable work, the terrain upon which one considered as conventional research and writing in the field of study had dramatically shifted, thereby expanding the boundaries of military history itself.[4]

Meanwhile, historians of the modern civil rights movement have traced the origins of the challenge to white supremacy back to the First World War and recent studies have mapped out the arc of black protest through the New Deal and World War Two eras.[5] Much of the work has used terminology such as "the long civil rights movement" to theorize about political militancy among national black leaders like A. Phillip Randolph and the March on Washington movement and Walter White and the National Association for the Advancement of Colored People as well as to describe a rich and expanding repertoire of civil rights activism during the period.[6] Other scholars such as Brenda Gayle Plummer, Penny Von Eschen, Mary Dudziak, and Carol Anderson have pointed toward the Cold War and the strategies waged by civil rights leaders to gain access to the most hallowed structures of power.[7] As a result, narratives of struggle were dramatically altered, setting in motion a veritable stream of new perspectives on civil rights and human rights struggle.

At the same time, new studies on black politics and activism of the late 1960s have followed hard on the heels of the long civil rights movement literature. Led by Charles Jones, Kathleen Cleaver, Komozi Woodard, Jeanne Theoharis, Yohuru Williams, and Peniel E. Joseph, scores of scholars have told stories about the black power movement that linked economic justice and urban reform to grassroots struggle and self-determination. Largely focused on Northern areas and situated in the late 1960s, this rich spate of literature has successfully pushed forth a nuanced, yet complex portraiture of the black freedom struggle.[8]

While labor unions, the black press, civil rights organizations and leaders, and human rights activists have held the attention of these streams of new scholarship, black freedom movements initiated after wearing the nation's uniform have gone largely unnoticed. Many studies have studied the civil rights activism of black soldiers at various points during America's wars throughout the twentieth century, but few have attempted to connect their postwar activism to the broader fabric of American life itself.[9] In fact, the thoughts and actions of the ex-GIs and the characteristics of struggle they shared with sectors of the black community have been kept as separate as the military's long-standing tradition, custom, and practice of racial segregation itself. With that, the political narratives that connect black veterans' struggles for equality after World War One through the Korean War and from the black nationalist movements during the Vietnam War to African American battles for freedom during the Persian Gulf Wars and how their postwar thoughts and activities of ex-GIs were deeply enmeshed in the broader themes surrounding the African American experience have remained hidden from public view.

This book, *Black Veterans, Politics, and Civil Rights in Twentieth-Century America: Closing Ranks*, gives voice to the silences within those bodies of literature. Following the lead of promising research in the New American Military History, the New Social History, and recent studies of the black freedom movement, it reassesses the connection between the wartime experiences of African American soldiers and their postwar political struggles for equality in American society. Beginning with World War One, Kevin Greene points out in "We Never Get to be Men" that African American veterans like William "Big Bill" Broonzy gained a new sense of manhood and an enlarged political consciousness born from their experiences in Europe with the institutional racism within the segregated army and their interactions with France's egalitarianism. Upon returning home, Broonzy left the Arkansas hinterland for the heady urban setting of Chicago, Illinois. There, the famed bluesman produced new melodic harmonies that articulated the lessons he learned while serving overseas as well as his new perception of American democratic ideals, giving new meaning to the "New Negro" movement. However, the blues that he created also reflected the tragic-comic resonances of frustration that he and other veterans would experience later throughout the rest of the 1920s. For many ex-GIs like Broonzy, their postwar lives would be indelibly marked by altruistic expectations of democratic concessions from the government that they had served so faithfully and the dashed hopes of collective and individual prosperity.

Moving from the turbulent decades of the Great Depression and New Deal era of the 1930s through the turbulent war-torn years of the 1940s, black ex-GIs drew upon their bittersweet military experiences to fashion a renewed sense of self. To be sure, black soldiers serving in the various branches of the armed forces were determined not to experience the broken promises of World War One. What's more, almost to a man and woman, they embraced the Double Victory imperatives asserted by African American leaders A. Phillip Randolph and Walter White and the self-determinative impulses of the Atlantic Charter espoused by the Allied powers and its leadership abroad. But the hard lessons of Jim Crow military discrimination had hardened the resolve of young black men who stood in the ranks during the period. Yet as they also discovered upon returning home, war and its nightmarish realities of death and injury raised new questions about race in America that could not be ignored. In "Frames Refocused," I explore the new outlook on race that blinded black and white veterans developed while recovering and readjusting to their injuries at Old Farms Convalescent Hospital in Avon, Connecticut, during the early 1940s. While withstanding a seemingly endless battery of rehabilitative phases on the road to recovery, they quickly discovered that the heavily wooded medical facility offered them an environment in which they could discuss, debate, and evaluate the racial conditions that shaped their lives in the years prior to their injury. Over time, the military hospital and school fostered among the uniformed individuals a deeper sense of racism in America and a new identity that was grounded largely in the life-altering experience of disability that they all shared. Such associations, forged from the ashes of war and death, would have lasting implications for ex-GIs and the militant progressive politics they expressed throughout the war and afterward.

For black Korean War veterans, the lessons of race and war provided the opening salvoes for a different "War within the War." As numerous ex-GIs of the war and future veterans of the emerging civil rights struggle in the 1950s and 1960s have attested, the years following the Second World War spelled the intensified struggle for a new meaning of military service, manhood, and equality. Selika M. Ducksworth-Lawton's story of the resistive measures waged by the Deacons for Defense and Justice (DDJ) to stem the racist activities of the Ku Klux Klan in the Deep South during the early 1960s provides a vivid window into how military service and the war in Korea framed the responses of the black community to the local powers that be. Largely eschewing a revolutionary nor progressive outlook, DDJ members rejected nonviolent direct-action strategies and took up arms to aid African American and white activists in areas in and around Bogalusa, Louisiana. Paying careful attention to geography and population density, Ducksworth-Lawton interrogates the notion that nonviolent and armed self-defense strategies sprang up separately in military and civilian spheres by rightfully asserting that both were deeply rooted in the lessons of the tactics black ex-GIs learned while wearing the nation's uniform. With that, a different picture of civil rights struggle emerges, one that alters the prism that has depicted the very contours of American democracy itself.[10]

Despite the integration of the armed forces and various areas of American society during the 1960s, racial discrimination in American life continued to mark the lives of those who entered military service. And in many ways, as Wallace Terry, David Parks, James Westheider, and John Sherwood have contended, black ex-GIs found that the troubles that plagued them in civil life and in the military were two sides of the same coin. Indeed, the themes of institutional racism, 1960s civil rights struggle, and alternative paths to equality, emerge in Jeremy P. Maxwell's study for this volume. In "The Military No More," Maxwell explores the odyssey that shaped the experiences of black service personnel throughout the American involvement in Vietnam during the period. Examining the trajectory of black perceptions to the racial problems in the Vietnam War military, he illuminates how their thoughts and actions paralleled the responses of the black community to the political and social changes of the 1960s. By the end of the decade, black Vietnam War–era veterans in the navy had fashioned a new conceptual framework for understanding the American military not just in Southeast Asia, but in other facets of American life altogether.[11]

America's involvement in the Persian Gulf Wars and Operations Desert Storm and Shield serve as the backdrop for Elizabeth Desnoyers-Colas's chapter. Vietnam, the disproportionate numbers of black service personnel in the nation's volunteer military, and the economic disparities that blacks faced in the civilian sphere engaged the energies and the attention of the African American press, congressional and religious clergy, and civil rights leaders throughout the country. But after African American women and men who served with marine corps, navy, and army units during the war returned home, they discovered that America's cease-fire with Iraq may have brought one phase of the conflict to a close for their generation, but also unwittingly opened a new front for the ongoing war for equality waged by America's black veterans at home. Thus, the American peace required a different relationship between African American veterans and the civil society, one that would continue to resonate with America's black ex-GIs well into the twenty-first century. All in all, her essay raises a new set of questions that future scholars must contemplate when thinking about the historical role that African American GIs have played in defense of the United States and the treacherous road the country has taken towards fulfilling the promise of democracy.

In many ways, Jacob Lawrence may have provided a pathway for future scholars to understand the military experiences of African Americans and how their wartime politics have intersected with civil rights struggle throughout the twentieth century. In late May of 1947, the noted visual artist and Guggenheim fellow produced a stark, yet beautiful black and white drawing titled *The Builders* that aptly spoke directly to the life and struggles of America's veterans. In the self-styled mural unveiled for a veteran's convention held in New York City, he depicts two figures, a black man and white man working together on a construction site. The black laborer is shown holding a plumb line; his white counterpart is wielding a hammer. When asked about the meaning of the drawing, Lawrence, a former navy seaman who served in World War Two, explained, "the figures of the two builders are symbolic of the movement developing among veterans of our country to build a new and better postwar world. *The Builders* shows us that veterans of both races must work together in achieving their common aims and purposes," he asserted.[12] If scholars are to realize the postwar future that he suggests, then we must at least contemplate the historical groundwork that he and other ex-GIs have laid out for us. Anything less would be extremely disappointing.

NOTES

1. Rayford W. Logan, "Introduction to the 1969 Reprint," *What the Negro Wants*, 3d ed. (Chapel Hill, NC: University of North Carolina Press, 1944; New York: Agathon Press, 1969, Notre Dame, IN: University of Notre Dame Press, 2001), xxxv. Citations are to the 2001 edition.

2. Kenneth R. Janken, *Rayford W. Logan and the Dilemma of the African-American Intellectual* (Amherst, MA: University of Massachusetts Press, 1993), ch. 2; Rayford W. Logan Papers, Diary 1940, Box 3, Manuscript Division, Library of Congress, Washington, DC.

3. Peter Karsten, *The Military in America: From the Colonial Period to the Present* (New York: The Free Press, 1980); Peter Karsten, "The 'New' American Military History: A Map of the Territory Explored and Unexplored," *American Quarterly* 36:3 (1984): 389–418; John W. Shy, *A People Numerous and Armed: Reflections on the Military Struggle for American Independence* (New York: Oxford University Press, 1976, revised; Ann Arbor: University of Michigan Press, 1990); Richard H. Kohn, "The Social History of the American Soldier: A Review and Prospectus for Research," *American Historical Review* 86:3 (June 1981): 553–67; Edward M. Coffman, "The New American Military History," *Military Affairs: The Journal of Military History* (January 1984): 1–5; John Whiteclay Chambers II, "The New Military History: Myth and Reality," *Journal of Military History* 55 (1991): 395–406; Robert M. Citino, "Military Histories Old and New: A Reintroduction," *The American Historical Review* 112:4 (October 2007): 1070–90. an important rejoinder to the new studies, please see John A. Lynn, "The Embattled Future of Academic Military History," *The Journal of Military History* 61 (1997): 777–89.

4. Wayne E. Lee, "Early American Ways of War: A New Reconnaissance, 1600–1815," *The Historical Journal* 44:1 (March 2001): 269–89; Mark Grimsley, "In Not So Dubious Battle: The Motivations of American Civil War Soldiers," *Journal of Military History* 62 (1998): 175–88; Elizabeth Fenn, "Beyond Jeffrey Amherst: Biological Warfare in Eighteenth-Century North America," *Journal of American History* 86 (2000): 1552–80.

5. Steven A. Reich, "Soldiers of Democracy: Black Texans and the Fight for Citizenship, 1917–1921," *Journal of American History* 82:4 (March 1996): 1478–1504; Winston James, *Holding Aloft the Banner of Ethiopia: Caribbean Radicalism in Early Twentieth-Century America* (London: Verso, 1999); Mark R. Schneider, *We Return Fighting: The Civil Rights Movement in the Jazz Age* (Boston: Northeastern University Press, 2002); Davarian L. Baldwin, *Chicago's New Negroes: Modernity, the Great Migration, and Black Urban Life* (Chapel Hill: University of North Carolina Press, 2007); Glenda E. Gilmore, *Defying Dixie: The Radical Roots of Civil Rights, 1919–1950* (New York: W. W. Norton, 2008); Chad L. Williams, *Torchbearers of Democracy: African American Soldiers in the World War I Era* (Chapel Hill: University of North Carolina Press, 2010).

6. For example, see Robert Korstad and Nelson Lichtenstein, "Opportunities Found and Lost: Labor, Radicals, and the Early Civil Rights Movement," *Journal of American History* 75 (December 1988): 786–811; John Egerton, *Speak Now Against the Day: The Generation Before the Civil Rights Movement in the South* (New York: Knopf, 1994); Patricia Sullivan, *Days of Hope: Race and Democracy in the New Deal Era* (Chapel Hill: University of North Carolina Press, 1996); Beth Thompkins Bates, "A New Crowd Challenges the Agenda of the Old Guard in the NAACP, 1933–1941," *American Historical Review* 102 (1997): 340–77; Robert R. Korstad, *Civil Rights Unionism: Tobacco Workers and the Struggle for Democracy in the Mid-Twentieth-Century South* (Chapel Hill: University of North Carolina Press, 2003); Martha Biondi, *To Stand and Fight: The Struggle for Civil Rights in Postwar New York City* (Cambridge, MA: Harvard University Press, 2003); Kevin Boyle, "Labor, the Left, and the Long Civil Rights Movement," *Social History* 30:3 (2005): 366–72; Darlene Clark Hine, "Black Professionals and Race Consciousness: Origins of the Civil Rights Movement, 1890–1950,"

Journal of American History 89, no. 4 (March 2003): 1279–94. The most cited work that has used the phraseology "long movement" in the literature is Jacquelyn Dowd Hall's provocative essay, "The Long Civil Rights Movement and the Political Uses of the Past," *Journal of American History* 91:4 (March 2005): 1233–63.

7. Brenda Gayle Plummer, *Rising Wind: Black Americans and U.S. Foreign Affairs, 1935–1960* (Chapel Hill: University of North Carolina Press, 1996); Penny M. Von Eschen, *Race against Empire: Black Americans and Anticolonialism, 1937–1957* (Ithaca, NY: Cornell University Press, 1997); Mary L. Dudziak, *Cold War Civil Rights: Race and the Image of American Democracy* (Princeton: Princeton University Press, 2000); Carol Anderson, *Eyes Off the Prize: The United Nations and the African American Struggle for Human Rights, 1944–1955* (New York: Cambridge University Press, 2000).

8. Charles E. Jones, ed., *The Black Panther Party (Reconsidered)* (Baltimore: Black Classic Press, 1998); Kathleen Cleaver and George Katsiaficas, eds., *Liberation, Imagination, and the Black Panther Party: A New Look at the Panthers and Their Legacy* (New York: Routledge, 2001); Jeanne Theoharis and Komozi Woodard, eds., *Freedom North: Black Freedom Struggles Outside the South, 1940–1980* (Durham: Duke University Press, 2006); Yohuru R. Williams, *In Search of the Black Panther Party* (Durham: Duke University Press, 2006); Peniel E. Joseph, "Black Liberation without Apology: Reconceptualizing the Black Power Movement," *Black Scholar* 31 (Fall–Winter 2001): 2–19; Peniel E. Joseph, *Waiting 'Til the Midnight Hour: A Narrative History of Black Power in America* (New York: Henry Holt and Company, 2006).

9. On black veterans' wartime activism and their contribution to postwar struggles for equality, see George Lipsitz, *A Life in the Struggle: Ivory Perry and the Culture of Opposition* (Philadelphia: Temple University Press, 1988); John Dittmer, *Local People: The Struggle for Civil Rights in Mississippi* (Urbana: University of Illinois Press, 1994); Charles Payne, *I've Got the Light of Freedom: The Organizing Tradition and the Mississippi Freedom Struggle* (Berkeley: University of California Press, 1995); Gail O'Brien, *The Color of Law: Race, Violence, and Justice in the Post–World War II South* (Chapel Hill: University of North Carolina Press, 1999); Timothy Tyson, *Radio Free Dixie: Robert F. Williams & The Roots of Black Power* (Chapel Hill: University of North Carolina Press, 1999); Lance E. Hill, *The Deacons for Defense: Armed Resistance and the Civil Rights Movement* (Chapel Hill: University of North Carolina Press, 2004); Christopher S. Parker, *Fighting for Democracy: Black Veterans and the Struggle against White Supremacy in the Postwar South* (Princeton: Princeton University Press, 2009); Adriane Lentz-Smith, *Freedom Struggles: African Americans and World War I* (Cambridge, MA: Harvard University Press, 2009); Chad L. Williams, *Torchbearers of Democracy: African American Soldiers in the World War I Era* (Chapel Hill: University of North Carolina Press, 2010); Jeffrey T. Sammons and John H. Morrow Jr., *Harlem's Rattlers and the Great War: The Undaunted 369th Regiment and the African American Quest for Equality* (Lawrence: University Press of Kansas, 2014).

10. For a sample of the importance that the Korean War had on a generation of civil rights activists in the postwar era, see Amiri Baraka, *Blues People* (New York: Random House, 1963); James Forman, *The Making of Black Revolutionaries* (New York: MacMillan, 1972); George Lipsitz, *A Life in the Struggle: Ivory Perry and the Culture of Opposition*; Charles Rangel, *And I Haven't Had a Bad Day Since: From the Streets of Harlem to the Halls of Congress* (New York: Thomas Dunne, 2007).

11. For several of the most incisive analysis of the struggles of black GIs during the Vietnam War decade, see David Parks, *G.I. Diary* (Washington, DC: Howard University Press, 1984); Wallace Terry, *Bloods: An Oral History of the Vietnam War by Black Veterans* (New York: Ballantine Books, 1984); James Westheider, *Fighting on Two Fronts: African Americans and the Vietnam War* (New York: New York University Press, 1997) and *The African American Experience in Vietnam: Brothers in Arms* (New York: Rowman & Littlefield, 2008); John D. Sherwood, *Black Sailor, White Navy: Racial Unrest in the Fleet During the Vietnam War Era* (New York: New York University Press, 2007).

12. "UNAVA Circular's Cover Drawn by Noted Painter," *Baltimore Afro-American* (May 24, 1947), 6.

Chapter One

"We Never Get to be Men"

Big Bill Broonzy, Black Consciousness, and WWI's Returning Black Veterans[1]

Kevin D. Greene

As a soldier of the Services of Supply for the American Expeditionary Force stationed in Brest, France, famous Chicago bluesman William "Big Bill" Broonzy transformed himself into something vastly different than the Arkansas sharecropper, country fiddler, and preacher he had been before the war who, "didn't want nobody tellin" him how to live his life.[2] Upon receiving his discharge from the U.S. Army at Camp Pike, near Little Rock, Arkansas, in 1919, Big Bill faced challenges to his newfound perspectives almost immediately. In Arkansas, he stepped off the train wearing his clean, crisp uniform with pride and dignity. Immediately, like countless other returning black veterans from the Great War, he received an embarrassing public beratement from an old, white plantation manager for whom he had once worked. In this pivotal moment, Bill's life would change forever. The exchange was powerful:

> I got off the train . . . I met a white fellow that I was knowin before I went to the Army. So he told me "Listen boy," "Now you been in the Army?" I told him "Yeah." He says, "How'd you like it?" I said, it's "O.K." He says, "Well . . . you ain't in the Army now." "And those clothes you got there . . . take'em home and get out of 'em and get you some overalls." "Because there's no nigger gonna walk around here with no Uncle Sam's uniform on up and down the streets."[3]

The man continued to direct Broonzy towards the local commissary where he could buy overalls and return to sharecropping's system of debt peonage. But the hardened and awakened veteran he had become was no longer indifferent to what was happening. Big Bill and thousands of African Americans throughout the United States were quickly learning of the dangers posed by transformed African American servicemen in uniform.

African American soldiers in World War I, at every level, served complex roles as members of the United States' American Expeditionary Force (AEF). Wherever they served and in whatever capacity, they transformed their experiences in the Great War into vehicles for combating human rights abuses and initiating fundamental political, social, and cultural change for the race. At every turn, whether as commissioned and noncommissioned laborers and combatants, black soldiers of the period faced Jim Crow segregation from the beginning of their training in army installments in the U.S. South to the battlefields and barracks of France through to their return to the United States. Of course, the American army in 1917 was completely segregated with separate divisions and units (like Services of Supply [SOS] or the famous 369th) for African Americans, and commanded, with the exception of very few black officers, almost completely by white men. Running through this segregated army was the quintessential belief that black troops were inherently inferior to whites in every capacity of soldiering. As a result, Jim Crow racism followed the AEF to Europe in 1918 and both civilian and senior leadership supported it. Stories of cruel treatment by white officers and calculated deference on behalf of the rare black officer, ensured that countless actions sparked from racial tensions—conscripted labor, substandard facilities, fighting, lynching, salacious rumors about black soldiers, trumped-up court-martials—became part of the institutionalized discrimination faced by black soldiers. At the same time, however, international travel, the trials of combat, the perceived absence of racism among French soldiers and civilians, and the patriotic dignity born of wartime service transformed their identity and manhood just enough to question their place in American democracy. Did the United States deserve the courage, honor, bravery, and sacrifice they gave so freely for a country more likely to embarrass or kill them in their uniforms than parade them as heroes? As they toiled with this dilemma, many black soldiers returned home determined more than ever to demand their rights as citizens rather than try to earn them. Big Bill Broonzy arrived in Arkansas in 1919, like tens of thousands of black veterans of the Great War, with a rapidly expanding black consciousness and emerging New Negro sensibilities.[4]

By the war's end, towering African American intellectual W.E.B. Du Bois recognized this realization would be a recurring phenomenon among returning black veterans when he wrote:

> They began to hate prejudice and discrimination as they had never hated it before. They began to realize its internal meaning and complications. Far from

filling them with a desire to escape from their race and country, they were filled with a bitter, dogged determination never to give up the fight for Negro equality in America . . . [a] new, radical Negro spirit has been born in France which leaves us older radicals far behind.[5]

Long before Big Bill left for military service, a lifetime of humiliating public spectacles and too close run-ins with extra-judicial, racialized violence in the river bottoms of the Arkansas Delta had instilled an inescapable contempt for his ancestral home and profoundly shaped his race consciousness. Broonzy once explained that his own recognition of what W.E.B. Du Bois described as "the veil" and "double consciousness," the moment "from when he could remember" until he "could understand what [his] people was saying" when he realized that he was African American in a foundationally racist society, occurred from a series of conversations he had shared with his mother as a child about the inherent dangers in associating with white women.[6] But his experience as a veteran of the Great War redefined what that "veil," the Deep South, and American democracy might be.[7]

Big Bill's early past is difficult to track. At his death in 1958, he had convinced the world that he was born in Scott, Mississippi, in 1893 and moved to Arkansas in 1900. Biographers have spent a decade trying to retrace Broonzy's story and have concluded that the erstwhile bluesman may in fact have been born in 1903 in and around Pine Bluff, Arkansas. The only definitive document discovered as proof is a family ledger listing the name Lee Bradley in 1903. While not an official legal document, the ledger brings into question many elements of Broonzy's past. Nevertheless, Alan Lomax, folklorist and longtime friend, met Big Bill's sister Laney sometime in the 1950s, who "produced certificates" documenting June 26, 1898, as Broonzy's actual birthday.[8]

The 1910 U.S. Census lists a Lee Bradley from Jefferson County, Arkansas, born in 1904, aged 6.[9] His death certificate from 1958 in Cook County, Chicago, lists 1893. Most of this back and forth with the details of his actual birth date has been used to prove or disprove Broonzy's proclaimed service in the American Expeditionary Force in WWI. If born in 1893 he would have been 24 when he entered the army, and if born in 1903, he would have been 14. Some have argued that at 14 he would have been too young to have actually served in the military, and, therefore, repeated stories of the Great War he had heard from friends and family members. This could stand as a plausible argument, except that countless Americans in times of war, including my own grandfather (age 16), have invariably lied about their age to serve their country. In this case, my book from which this chapter draws suggests that it is impossible to know the exact date, but firmly believes the veracity of his declaration of military service.

Nevertheless, Big Bill Broonzy was born Lee Conley Bradley on June 26, somewhere around the turn of the twentieth century in and around the Arkansas/Mississippi Delta, the fourth boy of ten children.[10] He grew up within a large, poor, and relatively stable sharecropping family with roots in slavery and the era of Reconstruction. By 1910, the family had moved to Lake Dick, Arkansas, a small community situated near the area of Jefferson County today known as Plum Bayou. This is repetitive. The 1900 census lists his father Frank Bradley, as a farmer, but ten years later as a porter in a local retail store, so Broonzy must have worked in and around farms throughout most of his childhood and adolescence.[11]

According to Broonzy, his first opportunity to leave Arkansas or the United States itself came during WWI. Broonzy entered the U.S. army in 1917. He received basic training at Camp Pike, Arkansas, then transported to Newport News, Virginia, and finally shipped off to Brest, France, as a member of the American Expeditionary Force in WWI. Between 1918 and 1919, Broonzy served in the U.S. Army, one of the 380,000 African Americans contributing to the nation's efforts in World War I.[12] Like many of his fellow black soldiers, Broonzy had witnessed both the horrors of war and the open racism that had followed the AEF from the United States to Europe, and he was forever changed by these experiences.[13]

Of course, the 160,000 African Americans stationed in Europe working in "supply companies" were forced to unload ships, build roads, dig ditches, bury the dead, deliver mail, lay railroad lines, and construct camps, what Big Bill called the "dirty work" of the military.[14] In some cases, for nearly sixteen hours a day, most black soldiers stationed with the Services of Supply worked in the same manner as southern gang and camp laborers back home.[15] Big Bill had worked in the aforementioned labor systems many times throughout his life, including "levee camps, extra gangs, road camps . . . rock camps and rock quarries."[16] He even lived within the unhealthy and disgusting conditions of the levee and railroad extra gang camps, where men "slept in the same clothes they worked in."[17] He learned a few things about life in barracks, having lived in labor camps and witnessed his colleagues whipped by "cat-o-nine-tails," drop dead from sheer exhaustion, cheated out of money because of their illiteracy, coerced into dangerous, life-threatening tasks, trapped by debt peonage, and threatened by prison or death if they dared argue against any of these humiliating and dehumanizing infractions. As it turns out, life in the military for black soldiers risking their lives to defend democracy shared similarities with the lives they had lived back home.

As Broonzy remembered, some officers recognized skilled laborers among his fellow black soldiers, but most believed that young African American conscripts "didn't know anything else to do."[18] Therefore, most of the members of the company "had that same old hard work [they] had at home."[19] In fact, most African American conscripts were never intended for use in combat on the front lines, as many racist military staff and draft board officials had predetermined black soldier's inability to serve in combat, thus relegating 80 percent of black soldiers to hard labor under the banner of making the world safe for democracy.[20] At the same time, black soldiers stationed in Europe faced harsh and cruel treatment from white soldiers and military police all too eager to remind blacks of their place in a segregated military and reinforce Jim Crow on foreign soil.

One of the twentieth century's premier historians, Rayford Logan, serving as a first lieutenant in Virginia's 372nd Infantry Regiment, sailed for France on March 30, 1918. Aboard the ship he quickly discovered the army's institutionalized racism when the regiment's commanding officer reassigned Logan and other black officers the worst staterooms and forced them to dine in segregated mess decks. Upon arriving in St. Naizarre, France, another important American point of entry just south of Brest, Lieutenant Logan was made to live in substandard, segregated housing and mandated to eat with black enlisted men. For the latter he and his fellow black officers were severely reproached for violating army officer regulations despite not having any other option.[21]

Noncommissioned officer, Sergeant Elijah "Ely" Green of the SOS, suffered both the inhumane demands for black labor on the docks of St. Naizarre as well as open racial violence from military police and marine guards. As a commander of a stevedore platoon, Green oversaw his men working sixteen-hour days—sometimes for weeks at a time—unloading ships and re-prepping them for their return voyages by African American soldiers without adequate clothing or supplies. Green recalled that even German prisoners suggested his men were little more than slaves, recognizing the brutal conditions and ragged appearances in which these servicemen labored. Confronting instances of racial violence against his men also became part of Sergeant Green's command. A black private from his squad was shot and killed by military police for venturing too close to a French prostitute. Another was stabbed with a bayonet by a marine for attempting to grab candy that had fallen to the deck from a busted storage container. For the latter infraction, Green's men tried to retaliate only to face a dozen and a half, armed and ready-to-fire, marines. As a result of the incident, Green and his men were arrested, beaten, and tortured. From that point forward, race and World War I held a completely new meaning for Ely Green.[22]

Like his black brothers-in-arms, Broonzy lived in strictly segregated barracks at camp and blacks were forbidden to enter the white area of the grounds. The white officers believed that "the germs" from the African American troops would infect the white soldier's camp, even though white soldiers were allowed to enter the black barracks and "shoot craps." One lieutenant, who Broonzy remembered as "tough," "didn't care what he said to a Negro or what happened . . . he'd always put the hardest things he could on a Negro."[23] The black soldiers stationed in France learned quickly that white officers would "punish them for nothing" and life was especially difficult for those who "stood up for their rights."[24]

Most black soldiers, particularly those in the SOS stationed in France, experienced horrific treatment by both white and black officers. African American laborers received unending physical, psychological, and emotional abuse. Passes for recreational time were infrequent and limited to incredibly small geographic spaces. White officers frequently banned African American troops from entering French towns in order to constrain their access to alcohol and, at all cost, prevent them from interacting with French women. Black commissioned and noncommissioned officers, viewing themselves as superior, professional (regular army) soldiers, occasionally expressed their disdain for draftees through acts of violence as well. Sergeant Ely Green witnessed the execution of a starving draftee, who happened to be late for chowtime. The underfed soldier reached for a piece of bread and was summarily shot multiple times by a black professional, noncommissioned officer acting as if he had just killed a "cockroach."[25] Combat units, too, experienced discrimination at the hands of U.S. Army leadership. The Ninety-second Division, for example, inadequately trained, poorly equipped, and led by many inept white officers, suffered heavy casualties between September 26 and October 1, 1918, during the first phase of the Meuse-Argonne offensive. Rather than admit fault, the division's high command blamed black officers for inefficiency and cowardice in the line of duty. Army courts-martial demanded the immediate dismissal of thirty officers and, although later exonerated, sentenced a few men to death for cowardice. As a result, the Ninety-second was labeled a failure and pulled from the front a little more than a week after it had arrived.[26]

Despite these harsh realities for black soldiers in WWI, Broonzy's anecdotes of life in the camps of France often reflected a more nuanced experience. He once recalled an incident involving a travel pass to town, six fellow black soldiers, twelve white soldiers, and a black cat. The superstitious black soldiers apparently had attempted to catch the cat in hopes of preventing a streak of bad luck in the middle of war-torn Europe, if the cat happened to cross their paths. So, as Broonzy told it, the six men set out to chase the cat for nearly two hours, screaming "don't let him cross," while the twelve white soldiers watched in befuddled guffaw.[27] Broonzy and company finally caught the cat, returned it to the proper side of the street, and continued into town to grab a few drinks, as the white soldiers returned to base. "From then on," Broonzy remembered, every time black and white soldiers crossed paths in the camp, the white soldiers began laughing at all black soldiers. After an extended period of time, the African American soldiers in the camp took offense to the laughter, as they thought the whites were laughing because the soldiers "were black."[28] As a result, the black soldiers crossed the imaginary color line in the camp to confront their white comrades, prompting the executive officers to inquire into what the escalating dustup was about. As a crowd of 1,000 soldiers gathered, one of the dozen white soldiers explained the story of the six black troops and the black cat, creating uproars of laughter in the camp that even caused the commanding officers to chuckle. "After that day," Broonzy remembered, "the white soldiers would come over and play games with us and for fourteen months everybody laughed about the night we catched the black cat."[29]

The story of the black cat is filled with racist overtones of life in the camps for black soldiers, but more importantly highlights Broonzy's reflection of his changing identity in what was no doubt a very difficult period for a young man who did not know where he was "more than a goat."[30] An important part of Broonzy's race consciousness centered on his ability to find humor and personal strength in difficult situations, often reflecting those sentiments in a quick turn of phrase or his next song. Through his wartime experience, Broonzy developed a sense of his own manhood and consciousness that could only stem from such a life-altering experience. Broonzy once told Alan Lomax:

> You see, after I went into the Army and come out of the Army I couldn't stand that way . . . Because when I went to the Army it was a dead cinch you had to keep clean in the Army . . . those people on levee camps they wear the same clothes or sleep in the same clothes . . . But in the Army you had to keep yourself clean, and when I went into the Army I had gotten used to that, keeping clean, and then when I went back, they would still want to put me back in one of those places and I couldn't stand it any more, see? Cause I stayed in their two years and I got used to that . . . And fact of the business, when I come back home they want to put me back in one of them camps or back one of them jobs like that, see? I couldn't stand that no more. I wanted to be clean, I wanted to be presentable and be around in public places and meet people and get along with people . . . And that's why I say it opened my eyes, you know, and let me know that people could be human beings, not beasts.[31]

In a sense, Broonzy found in military service a dutiful and heroic opportunity to serve his country, and his experiences roused his growing contempt for a Jim Crow system that had emasculated black manhood and crippled black participation in American civic institutions. Even if black stevedores on the docks of Brest and St. Nizairre were treated like conscripted labor rather than soldiers, international travel, new forms of education, uniforms, decent meals, access to health care, and the knowledge of serving their country in a time of war created a sense of dignity and manliness that could never develop for someone like Broonzy in the Jim Crow South. In effect, through their experiences as soldiers in France, these black men imagined, at least in part, a world without Jim Crow oppression. For other African American soldiers, the institutionalized, oppressive racism in the AEF politicized a new black masculinity centered on a strong desire to demand civic equality over their own social parity. These soldiers had challenged the military's—and by association the U.S.'s—racist, discriminatory practices in Europe by disobeying orders, stealing provisions, sneaking out at night to visit French women, getting drunk, filing formal complaints, and shirking their work. Their frustrations with active service fostered a new masculinity and consciousness based on challenging America's racial status quo, wherever they found it in their communities, in the name of full participation in American democracy, even if it destroyed their livelihoods or killed them. Like many of his fellow black soldiers, Broonzy had witnessed both the horrors of war and the open racism that had followed the AEF from the United States to Europe and was forever changed by these experiences.[32]

For many Americans, the presence of black veterans in uniform returning to their homes across the country signified eminent danger to the power of Jim Crow and especially in the segregated South. Notorious segregationist and Mississippi governor Theodore Bilbo wrote an editorial picked up by the *Chicago Defender* in the summer of 1919, striking right to the heart of Southern segregationists' deepest fears.

> There is considerable feeling and bitter resentment on the part of the white people of the South brought about by the attempt of the Negro Race to seek social and political equality. The desire on the part of the Negro seems to have increased since the world war by the social reception and familiarity with Negro soldiers by a certain class of white women in France . . . This is strictly a white man's country, with a white man's civilization, and any dream on the part of the Negro Race to share social and political equality will be shattered in the end. If the Northern Negro lover wants to stop Negro lynching in the South, they must first get right the conception of the proper relationship that must necessarily exist between the races . . . [33]

These returning servicemen, like Broonzy, Logan, and Green, "contributed to a volatile social, political, and economic climate," which spawned an enormous growth of clashes in racial humiliation, violence, and public lynchings.[34] Black newspapers across the country, immediately following the war, featured columns and editorials filled with outrage and disgust at whites' beliefs that "these Negroes who have been in the camps and across the seas will 'forget their places' . . . and be well to have to them get rid of the uniform."[35]

Black Alabaman sharecropper Ned Cobb reflected on the irony of black veterans returning home to the South who had fought for democracy only to be publicly humiliated and assaulted upon their arrival. Cobb remembered:

> The colored man goin over there fightin, well, the white man holds his ground over here when comes back, he's the same . . . he ain't recognized more than a dog. In other words, it's the same for him, too, as it was before he went. What did they do to the niggers after the first world war? Meet em at these stations where they was getting off, comin back into the United States, and cut the buttons and armaments off of their clothes, make em get out of them clothes, make em take them uniforms off and they didn't have another suit of clothes—quite naturally, if they was colored they was poor and might not a had a thread of clothes in the world but them uniforms—make em walk in their underwear. . . . You a damn nigger right on, didn't give you no credit for what you done.[36]

It seems impossible to know if these instances of racial antagonism were surprising to returning veterans from the Deep South like Broonzy. What remains clear, is that these open intimidations and threats of racial violence would not go unchallenged. As he later recalled, "That's why I didn't never stay in the South no more after I come outta the Army . . . I couldn't stand that bossing around by anybody."[37] Clearly, the combination of Broonzy's southern roots, military service, and international experiences galvanized his disgust for the U.S.'s racial status quo and remapped his own consciousness. Like tens of thousands of returning black brothers-in-arms, he held a completely new understanding of race and the plight of African Americans in the southern United States. Once the memory of black life in the Deep South forged with those from his recent participation in the American Expeditionary Force in Europe, he quickly developed seemingly New Negro perspectives on race in the United States.[38]

Historian Chad Williams has suggested African American veterans of WWI "embodied a 'reconstructed' Negro, radicalized at the levels of racial, gender, and political consciousness by the combination of war and the ferocity of white supremacy."[39] Broonzy knew that the life he led after the army forced him to relinquish control to the white overseer that managed his tenant farm, to his wife at the time, who demanded that he improve their lot in life, and most of all, to the U.S. government—the institution that asked him to serve and, if need be, die abroad while refusing to guarantee his rights at home. Broonzy knew quite well that black men in the South "never get to be men . . . it's always boy until you get too old, then they called you uncle."[40] Broonzy once admitted that after returning home his personal life would never be the same.

> Well my wife always, before I went into the Army, whatsoever she said went. An when-after I went into the Army and came out, well, then she wanted to do the same thing, you know . . . Well I wouldn't stand for that, see? And the same things about a white man down there I had to work for. They'd try to tell me this and tell me that, and I didn't care no more about a white man than I did

about a black man, see? And whensoever he tried to tell me something that I had to do, why, that's why we fell out.[41]

Broonzy further explained to Lomax that Gertrude had wanted him to leave farming and join the difficult, but lucrative work on an extra gang for railroad companies.[42] Of course, he knew that most white employers, whether on tenant and sharecropping farms or levee and railroad gangs, gave little value, if any, to African American laborers' lives.[43]

All African Americans from the Deep South knew the dangers of working on levee camps, road crews, and extra railroad gangs, as any of these ventures were often conveyors to southern prisons or death.[44] Broonzy's older brother James, for example, drowned in a horrific revetment accident while working on the Arkansas River in Pine Bluff. An April 14, 1919, piece in the *Pine Bluff Commercial* indicated that on April 10, an unidentified white male had fallen alongside of James, as the barge upon which they were working suddenly listed and ejected both men into the Arkansas River. The anonymous white man was of course saved, but Bradley, "paralyzed with fear," could not accept the offered help and disappeared to the bottom of the river. Five days later, his body was discovered and identified as James Bradley and later buried near the family's home.[45] Once again, Broonzy was reminded of the disparaging world of the Jim Crow South, as his brother's life was sacrificed so that a white man's could be spared.

No evidence exists that might reveal why Broonzy left Arkansas for Chicago. His growing New Negro consciousness, his disillusionment with his marriage, the lifelong humiliations forced on blacks by the Jim Crow South, and the overall contempt for his condition, when combined with the death of his brother, may have pushed him over the edge. Broonzy lamented:

> Well the main reason I left from home because I couldn't stand the way that the white man had been treating me. I was just dumb to the fact; I thought it was the right way to be treated. And when I found out it was the wrong way to be treated, I just wouldn't take that no more . . . That's from me being in the Army . . . And fact of the business, after I found out that was more of the world than just Arkansas . . . and other people living in other parts of the world and was doing a durn sight better than I was doin . . . So I said "what the heck . . . Down here a man ain't nothing now how."[46]

Perhaps he became involved in a life-threatening altercation that forced him to run, but little evidence exists of any event of that nature and he never discussed that possibility with anyone. What does exist as evidence—his military service, his loathing of southern black labor systems, his knowledge of Chicago's Bronzeville through family connections and smuggled copies of the *Chicago Defender*, an overbearing wife, public humiliation in his uniform—had transformed Big Bill's identity into one that could no longer live under the weight of Jim Crow. Other bluesmen, like Riley "B. B." King, for example, left his Indianola, Mississippi, home in the middle of the night in 1945 after severely damaging the smokestack of the tractor he operated for a local planation. Scared of violent retribution, he ran from his wife and home in Mississippi for Memphis with a guitar and $2.50 in his pocket, never to return.[47] Like King, the themes presented in his life in the Deep South would become fodder for Broonzy's songwriting for decades. Broonzy would hint at the bevy of emotions he felt leaving home in one of his most famous compositions and recognized songs, "Key to the Highway."

> I got the key to the highway
>
> I'm gonna leave here runnin'
>
> 'Cause walkin' is most too slow
>
> I'm goin' down on the border
>
> Now where I'm better known
>
> 'Cause woman you don't do nothin'
>
> But drive a good man
>
> 'way from home

Late at night in January of 1921, hearing "a freight a coming," Big Bill Broonzy left Arkansas for good and "hoboed from there into St. Louis."[48] For around one month, Broonzy "got a little job there," saved up a few dollars, and on February 8, "wound up in Chicago."[49] Big Bill arrived at the Illinois Central Station, at 135 E. 11th Place, or more commonly known as the "Twelfth Street Station," perhaps arriving on Illinois Central Railroad's most flaunted locomotive, the Panama Limited,[50] which traveled daily from St. Louis to Chicago. Quickly, he made Chicago's Black Belt his home, several known Chicago addresses for Broonzy from 1930 to 1946 place him and his family in the city's South Side black belt: on Washburne Avenue in 1930, on West Washington Boulevard in 1944, and on South Parkway in 1946 and at his death.[51] In reality, Broonzy was but one American from the approximately twenty-nine million Southerners who left the South for opportunities in the North, Midwest, and West during the twentieth century. He arrived in Chicago as a country fiddler from rural Arkansas with developing New Negro sensibilities concerning the plight of African Americans in the Jim Crow South at a critical moment in the city's history.

Like tens of thousands of other southern migrants, Big Bill settled in Chicago with deep roots in his southern past but wanting desperately to move beyond its often-weighty grasp. Quickly, the blues queens of the early blues craze transformed Chicago into one of the most important music cities in the nation. Broonzy, already a professional musician in the South, would immediately engage with the ubiquitous and potent musical environment that Chicago still is today. But before he could fully engage the city's vibrant cultural constructs, he first had to learn to navigate urban life with his growing consciousness, amidst a city fully engaged in its own New Negro Renaissance.

In part, the emergence of the New Negro movement in Chicago centered on public negotiations between older generations of black Chicagoans and newly arriving migrants and their respective ideas about community respectability, black cultural creativity, and a new kind of entrepreneurialism rooted in commercialized leisure. New migrants, in the minds of the established black middle class, reinforced white notions of black inferiority by developing new identities formed within Bronzeville's public spaces and vibrant nightlife. This dimension nurtured a new identity in the emerging black urban consciousness that involved, in equal parts, southern cultural pathways and new ones inspired the city. A new generation of young black men and women discovered in black Chicago's cabarets, sporting dens, rent party circuits, dance halls, vaudeville houses, and movie theaters a world of leisure that remapped ideas about New Negro sensibilities. The fact that Chicago at the time was a heavily segregated city meant that much of this activity happened beyond the influence of whites in a manner that could never happen in the South. Not only did these spaces transform black consciousness and its relationship to black labor, it provided work within the black community in which African Americans could advance economically and express themselves artistically and physically, while simultaneously displaying pride in their community, the black aesthetic, and entrepreneurship. For Chicago New Negroes like Big Bill, the blues as part of the black consumer marketplace and community identity was not problematic for black Chicago's emerging New Negro leadership, but rather offered vibrancy and vitality to Bronzeville as a site for New Negro prescience and imagination.[52]

Rent parties, for example, became vessels for the development of black pop music and New Negro musicians' identities in black Chicago. As Langston Hughes recalled, he frequented many rent party flats:

> Where God knows who lived—because the guests seldom did—where the piano would be augmented by a guitar, or an old clarinet, or somebody with a pair of drums walking in off the street. And where awful bootleg whisky [prohibition was on] and good fried fish or steaming chitterlings were sold at very low prices. And the dancing and singing and impromptu entertaining went on until dawn came in at the windows.[53]

Rent parties allowed for the collectivization of the experiences of new migrants like Broonzy, while at the same time, introducing younger musicians like Big Bill to big-name celebrities—Blind Lemon Jefferson and Bessie Smith—in town to record, perform, and party in private homes. Until the repeal of prohibition, buffet flats and rent parties were, in some cases, the only venues for performance for upstarts like Broonzy. By befriending individuals with established ties to Chicago's blues culture at rent parties, Broonzy expected to both learn their music and take advantage of their connections within the city's growing music industry. As a representative of Chicago's New Negroes, Broonzy revealed the powerful contestations over "self-control, self-definition, and self-determination" that defined how the blues as a form of black popular music for black audiences would transmit across class and race boundaries in the twentieth century.[54]

Yet, New Negro ideologies varied widely among returning veterans. Lieutenant Rayford Logan, Sergeant Ely Green, and Private Lee Bradley (Big Bill Broonzy) followed different pathways after the end of the Great War, but each man shared one fundamental idea—racism and segregation in a supposedly "free" country was, in fact, an abomination. All three would experience unique successes following their ultimate decision to no longer accept Jim Crow discrimination. Lieutenant Rayford Logan, for example, used his service and training as a black solider in France to work as an organizer and interpreter in the growing pan-African movement. Discrimination in the military had sparked a burning fire within him. For the remainder of his life, Logan's New Negro transformation led to a long career focused on stamping out racism, hatred, and hypocrisy in the United States and beyond its borders. After the war, Logan remained in Europe and followed his growing multinational, New Negro perspectives by becoming the secretary for the Pan African Congress and helping W.E.B. Du Bois organize conferences in England, France, and Spain. He did not stop there.

In 1924, Logan returned to the United States and began a teaching career at one of Virginia's historically black colleges. In 1930, he enrolled in Harvard's doctoral program in history and became one of only a few African Americans at that point to earn a PhD (1936) from the prestigious university.[55] At Harvard, he studied pan-Africanism and the diplomatic relationship between the United States and Haiti. Howard University hired Logan in 1938 as a junior professor where he stayed for nearly four decades, serving as chair and distinguished professor in the Department of History. Moreover, as an intellectual and academic, Logan became an integral cog in Carter Woodson's Association for the Study of Negro Life and History and its Negro History Week campaigns. He still stands as one of twentieth-century America's leading black intellectuals. His mission as a man and an academic centered on uncovering the contradictions inherent in American democracy and diasporic pan-Africanism. His life's long journey for equality and black recognition began in France in 1918.[56]

Sargent Ely Green left the war and moved back to Texas, his adopted home state. Before his tour in France, he fled his native Tennessee in 1912 to evade being lynched and drifted from town to town looking for work to make a living. After the war, like Broonzy in Arkansas, Green could only stomach a few years in Texas. He had seen a lifetime of Jim Crow segregation, police brutality, and extrajudicial violence at the hands of southern whites and the U.S. Army, and could no longer tolerate the South's system of apartheid. Around the mid-1920s, he followed tens of thousands of black migrants along the path of the Great Migration, eventually settling in southern California. Once in California, Green worked on pleasure yachts as a valet so he could travel the world, ultimately visiting Mexico, Australia, Paraguay, Brazil, and Argentina. In the 1930s, he worked as a private caterer in Beverley Hills for Hollywood celebrities including Jon Barrymore and Mary Pickford. During World War II, Ely Green joined the massive wartime industries effort for southern California's Lockheed Corporation. While there, he attempted to desegregate one of their manufacturing plants in an organized civil and labor rights campaign. Although the program failed because of organized labor's refusal to integrate, Green was proud to again serve his country while simultaneously fighting for equal rights. Although he retired in the 1960s, Green would go on to write an autobiography published and reprinted by academic presses revealing his evolving identity and consciousness. He, too, returned from war a re-invented man.[57]

From the mid-1920s through the 1940s, recorded blues and live performances infused nearly every segment of black life in Chicago from Maxwell Street to South State Street and became an irreplaceable part of Chicago's cultural and social history. As both a veteran of the AEF and black southern migrant fed up with the Jim Crow South, Big Bill's growing black consciousness helped wipe clean his Arkansas past and refashion his identity as an urbane, upwardly mobile black artist and New Negro of Bronzeville. Big Bill is now considered one of the best and most important bluesmen in history as a guitarist, vocalist, and songwriter, and heralded as an international celebrity who took the blues to Europe following World War II. Only after the New Negro Renaissance waned in the early 1940s would Broonzy shed the carefully crafted, cosmopolitan image he constructed as one of the nation's most successfully recorded and accomplished blues celebrities of the period. Big Bill Broonzy transformed himself into a New Negro, cultural architect, and community leader under these auspices, and for the remainder of his life he would argue that his service in the Great War was the catalyst.[58]

Black veterans of the Great War, like the three men in this essay, returned to the United States with deeply developed understandings of their place within America's contradictory systems of democracy and Jim Crow segregation. Through their service in the U.S. Army, these black veterans evolved into worldly citizens no longer unaware of global blackness or other worlds beyond U.S. racism. In whatever manner they chose to express it—blues music, the academy, Hollywood—these black GIs came back from Europe with much broader definitions of black consciousness nestled in the evolving impact of the New Negro in black life. Big Bill Broonzy, like thousands of black veterans of the Great War "returned home from fighting," a proud, determined, and strong black man ready to "return fighting" and wield his music as a powerful weapon.[59]

PRIMARY SOURCES

Newspapers:

Chicago Defender 1919
Cleveland Gazette 1919
Kansas City Advocate 1919
Pine Bluff Commercial 1919
Pine Bluff Daily Graphic 1919
Savannah Tribune 1919
Savannah Tribune 1919
Topeka Plaindealer 1919
Washington Bee 1919

Government Documents and Collections:

1910 United States Census
1930 United States Census
Alan Lomax Collection, American Folklife Center, Library of Congress
Alan Lomax interview with Big Bill Broonzy, 03/02/1947. *Blues in the Mississippi Night Recordings,* Association for Cultural Equity
Illinois Office of Cook County Clerk, File 2405936
Pullman Company Archive, Newberry Library, Chicago, Illinois

SECONDARY SOURCES

Blackmon, Douglas A. *Slavery By Another Name: The Re-enslavement of Black Americans From the Civil War to World War II.* New York: Doubleday Books 2008.
Broonzy, Bill. *Big Bill Blues: William Broonzy's Story as told to Yannick Bruynoghe.* New York: De Capo Press, 1992.
Downey, Clifford J. *Images of Rail: Chicago and the Illinois Central Railroad.* Chicago: Arcadia Publishing, 2007.
Du Bois, W.E.B. *The Souls of Black Folk.* Chicago: A.C. McClurg & Co., 1903.
———. "An Essay Toward a History of Black Men in the Great War," *The Crisis* 18 (1919): 72.
———. "Returning Soldiers," *The Crisis* 18 (1919): 13.
Ellis, Mark. "'Closing Ranks' and 'Seeking Honors': W.E.B. Du Bois in World War I," *Journal of American History* 79, no.1 (1992): 96–124.
———. "W.E.B. Du Bois and the Formation of Black Opinion in World War I: A Commentary on 'The Damnable Dilemma,'" *Journal of American History* 81, no.1 (1995): 1584–90.
Franklin, John Hope. "Rayford Whittingham Logan (1897–1982)," *Hispanic American Historical Review* 63, no. 3 (1983): 596–97.
Green, Ely. *Ely: Too Black, Too White.* Amherst: University of Massachusetts Press, 1970.

Green, Ely, and Lillian Smith. *Ely: An Autobiography*. Athens, GA: University Press of Georgia, 2004.
Greene, Kevin D. *The Invention and Reinvention of Big Bill Broonzy*. Chapel Hill: University of North Carolina Press, 2018.
Harold, Ellen, and Peter Stone. "Big Bill Broonzy," *The Association for Cultural Equity*. Accessed April 20, 2016. http://www.culturalequity.org/alanlomax/ce_alanlomax_profile_broonzy.php.
House, Roger. *Blue Smoke: The Recorded Journey of Big Bill Broonzy*. Baton Rouge: Louisiana State University Press, 2009.
Jordan, William. "'The Damnable Dilemma': African-American Accommodation and Protest during World War I," *Journal of American History* 81, no.1 (1995): 1562–83.
Keene, Jennifer D. "W.E.B Du Bois and the Wounded World: Seeking Meaning in the First World War for African Americans," *Peace & Change* 26 (April 2001): 135–52.
King, B.B. *Blues All Around Me: The Autobiography of B.B. King*. New York: Avon Books, 1986.
Lentz-Smith, Adriane. *Freedom Struggles: African Americans and World War I*. Cambridge, MA: Harvard University Press, 2009.
Lewis, David Levering. *W.E.B. Du Bois: Biography of Race, 1868–1919*. New York: Owl Books, 1993.
———. *W.E.B. Du Bois: The Fight for Equality and the American Century, 1919–1963*. New York: Henry Holt & Company, 2000.
Lomax, Alan. "I Got The Blues," *Common Ground* 8, no. 4 (1948): 38–52.
———. *The Land Where the Blues Began*. New York: Doubleday Books, 1993.
Mjagkij, Nina. *Loyalty in Time of Trial: The African American Experience during World War I*. Lanham, MD: Rowman & Littlefield Publishers, 2011.
Riesman, Bob. *I Feel So Good: The Life and Times of Big Bill Broonzy*. Chicago: The University of Chicago Press, 2011.
Rosengarten, Theodore. *All God's Dangers: The Life of Nate Shaw*. New York: Alfred A. Knopf, 1974.
Simmons, Jefferey T. *Harlem's Rattlers and the Great War: The Undaunted 369th Regiment and the African America Quest for Equality*. Lawrence, KS: University Press of Kansas, 2014.
Slotkin, Richard. *Lost Battalions: The Great War and the Crisis of American Nationality*. New York: Henry Holt and Company, 2005.
Williams, Chad L. *Torchbearers of Democracy: African American Soldiers in the World War I Era*. Chapel Hill: The University of North Carolina Press, 2010.
Jenkin, Kenneth Robert. *Rayford W. Logan and the Dilemma of the African American Intellectual*. Amherst: The University of Massachusetts Press, 1993.

NOTES

1. This piece is an excerpt from chapter 1 of my book, *The Invention and Reinvention of Big Bill Broonzy*, from the University of North Carolina Press.

2. Alan Lomax Collection, Folder 09.04.10, American Folklife Center, Library of Congress. This collection holds several transcribed interviews with Lomax and Big Bill dating from 1947 to 1952, which Lomax featured in publications throughout his career. See Lomax, "I Got the Blues," *Common Ground* 8, no. 4 (1948): 38–52; *The Land Where the Blues Began* (New York: Doubleday Books, 1993).

3. Alan Lomax Collection, American Folklife Center, Library of Congress, Folder 09.04.10.

4. Adriane Lentz-Smith, *Freedom Struggles: African Americans and World War I* (Cambridge, MA: Harvard University Press, 2009); Nina Mjagkij, *Loyalty in Time of Trial: The African American Experience during World War I* (Lanham, MD: Rowman & Littlefield Publishers, 2011); Jefferey T. Sammons, *Harlem's Rattlers and the Great War: The Undaunted 369th Regiment and the African American Quest for Equality* (Lawrence, KS: University Press

of Kansas, 2014); Richard Slotkin, *Lost Battalions: The Great War and the Crisis of American Nationality* (New York: Henry Holt and Company, 2005); Chad L. Williams, *Torchbearers of Democracy: African American Soldiers in the World War I Era* (Chapel Hill: University of North Carolina Press, 2010); Mark Whalan, *The Great War and the Culture of the New Negro* (Gainesville: University Press of Florida, 2008).

5. W.E.B. Du Bois, "An Essay Toward a History of Black Men in the Great War," *Crisis* 18 (1919): 72.

6. W.E.B. Du Bois, *The Souls of Black Folk* (Chicago: A.C. McClurg & Co., 1903), 2–3; Lomax, Alan, "Paris: Big Bill Broonzy Interview," 05/13/1952, *Association for Cultural Equity*.

7. Since the 1990s, scholars investigating Du Bois' wrestling with the meaning of the black experience in WWI have highlighted his shifting approaches before, during, and after the war. See Mark Ellis, "'Closing Ranks' and 'Seeking Honors': W.E.B. Du Bois in World War I," *Journal of American History* 79 (June 1992): 96–124; David Levering Lewis, *W.E.B. Du Bois: Biography of a Race, 1868–1919* (New York: Owl Books, 1993), 528–74; William Jordan, "'The Damnable Dilemma': African-American Accommodation and Protest during World War I," *Journal of American History* 81 (March 1995): 1562–83; Mark Ellis, "W.E.B. Du Bois and the Formation of Black Opinion in World War I: A Commentary on 'The Damnable Dilemma,'" *Journal of American History* 81 (March 1995): 1584–90; David Levering Lewis, *W.E.B. Du Bois: The Fight for Equality and the American Century, 1919–1963* (New York: Henry Holt & Company, 2000), 58-60; Jennifer D. Keene, "W.E.B Du Bois and the Wounded World: Seeking Meaning in the First World War for African Americans," *Peace & Change* 26 (April 2001): 135–52; Chad L. Williams, *Torchbearers of Democracy: African American Soldiers in the World War I Era* (Chapel Hill: University of North Carolina Press, 2010).

8. Ellen Harold, and Peter Stone, "Big Bill Broonzy" *The Association for Cultural Equity*. Accessed 04/20/2016. http://www.culturalequity.org/alanlomax/ce_alanlomax_profile_broonzy.php.

9. 1910 U.S. census, Arkansas, Jefferson County digital image, Ancestry.com, accessed April 18, 2015, http://ancestory.com.

10. See Alan Lomax Collection, Folder 09.04.10, American Folklife Center, Library of Congress; 1910 U.S. Census; Ellen Harold and Peter Stone, "Big Bill Broonzy," *The Association for Cultural Equity*. Accessed 04/20/2016. http://www.culturalequity.org/alanlomax/ce_alanlomax_profile_broonzy.php; Roger House, *Blue Smoke: The Recorded Journey of Big Bill Broonzy* (Baton Rouge: Louisiana State University Press, 2009); Bob Riesman, *I Feel So Good: The Life and Times of Big Bill Broonzy* (Chicago: The University of Chicago Press, 2011), 1–5; Illinois Office of Cook County Clerk, File 2405936.

11. 1910 U.S. Census.

12. Big Bill's military records were destroyed in the 1973 fire that gutted the National Archives' military service records of U.S. Army veterans from WWI to the 1960s. What about the muster rolls for the black units that served in World War One? For more on this, please consult Emmett J. Scott's *Official History of the American Negro in World War* (1919).

13. Alan Lomax Collection, Folder 09.04.10, American Folklife Center, Library of Congress; Big Bill Broonzy, *Big Bill Blues: William Broonzy's Story as Told to Yannick Bruynoghe* (New York: De Capo Press, 1992), 37–38.

14. Ibid.

15. Williams, *Torchbearers of Democracy*, 110–13.

16. Alan Lomax, "Blues in the Mississippi Night Interviews," 03/02/1947, *Association for Cultural Equity*.

17. Alan Lomax, "Blues in the Mississippi Night Interviews," 03/02/1947, *Association for Cultural Equity*.

18. Alan Lomax Collection, Folder 09.04.10, American Folklife Center, Library of Congress.

19. Ibid.

20. Lentz-Smith, *Freedom Struggles*, 111–13; Williams, *Torchbearers of Democracy*, 53–55.

21. Williams, *Torchbearers of Democracy*, 128–29.

22. Lentz-Smith, *Freedom Struggles*, 124–27.
23. Alan Lomax interview with Big Bill Broonzy, 03/02/1947. *Blues in the Mississippi Night Recordings,* Association for Cultural Equity.
24. Williams, *Torchbearers of Democracy*, 110–13.
25. Ely Green, *Ely: Too Black, Too White* (Amherst: University of Massachusetts Press, 1970), 360.
26. Nina Mjagkij, *Loyalty in Time of Trial*, 100–102, 112–13; Williams, *Torchbearers of Democracy*, 138–40.
27. Alan Lomax interview with Big Bill Broonzy, 03/02/1947. *Blues in the Mississippi Night Recordings,* Association for Cultural Equity.
28. Ibid.
29. Alan Lomax interview with Big Bill Broonzy, 03/02/1947.
30. Alan Lomax Collection, Folder 09.04.10, American Folklife Center, Library of Congress.
31. Alan Lomax Collection, Folder 09.04.10, American Folklife Center, Library of Congress.
32. Williams, *Torchbearers of Democracy*, 261–65.
33. *Chicago Defender*, July 12, 1919, p. 1, found in Mjagkij, *Loyalty in Time of Trial*, 192.
34. Williams, *Torchbearers of Democracy*, 225.
35. "The Old and the New," *Washington Bee*, January 11, 1919; "Dr. R. R. Moton's Mission Abroad," *Cleveland Gazette*, February 8, 1919; "Decatur County Welcomes Soldiers," *Savannah Tribune*, April 26, 1919; "Kansas City, MO., Mayor Backs up for Dynamiters," *Topeka Plaindealer*, May 9, 1919; "American Negroes Unite Against Evil of Lynching," *Kansas City Advocate*, July 11, 1919; "Racial Clashes," *Savannah Tribune*, July 26, 1919; "Rev. S.E.J. Watson Speaks Before White Minsters Union," *Topeka Plaindealer*, December 19, 1919.
36. Theodore Rosengarten, *All God's Dangers: The Life of Nate Shaw* (New York: Alfred A. Knopf, 1974), 161.
37. Alan Lomax Collection, Folder 09.04.10, American Folklife Center, Library of Congress.
38. Williams, *Torchbearers of Democracy*, 263–64.
39. Ibid., 263.
40. Alan Lomax Collection, Folder 09.04.10, American Folklife Center, Library of Congress.
41. Alan Lomax Collection, Folder 09.04.10, American Folklife Center, Library of Congress.
42. Ibid.
43. Alan Lomax interview with Big Bill Broonzy, 03/02/1947. *Blues in the Mississippi Night Recordings,* Association for Cultural Equity.
44. Douglas A. Blackmon, *Slavery by Another Name: The Re-enslavement of Black Americans from the Civil War to World War II* (New York: Doubleday Books, 2008).
45. "Negro Drowns While Working on Revetment," *Pine Bluff Commercial*, April 4, 1919; "Fail to Find Body of Negro," *Pine Bluff Daily Graphic*, April 15, 1919; "Body of Negro Who Drowned Thursday Recovered Today," *Pine Bluff Commercial*, April 15, 1919; "Recover Body of Jim Bradley," *Pine Bluff Daily Graphic*, April 16, 1919. See Riesman, *I Feel So Good*, 272.
46. Alan Lomax Collection, Folder 09.04.10, American Folklife Center, Library of Congress.
47. B. B. King, *Blues All Around Me: The Autobiography of B. B. King* (New York: Avon Books, 1986), 93–95.
48. Alan Lomax Collection, Folder 09.04.10, American Folklife Center, Library of Congress.
49. Ibid.
50. The Illinois Central Railroad operated its New Orleans to Chicago service on the Panama Limited from 1911–1971 and the train has been memorialized in blues culture by numerous songs referring to its legendary run. See Clifford J. Downey, *Images of Rail: Chicago and the Illinois Central Railroad* (Chicago: Arcadia Publishing, 2007), 35–56.

51. 1930 U.S. Census, Cooke County, Chicago; *Pullman Company Archive*, Collection 06/02/03, Box 194, Newberry Library, Chicago, Illinois; Alan Lomax Collection, Folder 09.04.10, American Folklife Center, Library of Congress; Broonzy's death certificate is dated 08/17/1958 and lists 4706 S. Parkway as his address. See, Illinois Office of Cook County Clerk; File 2405936.

52. Davarian L. Baldwin, *Chicago's New Negroes: Modernity, The Great Migration and Black Urban Life* (Chapel Hill: University of North Carolina Press, 2007), 19.

53. Arna Bontemps and Langston Hughes, eds. *The Book of Negro Folklore* (New York: Dodd, Mead, 1958), 596–600.

54. Baldwin, "Introduction: New Negroes Forging a New World," 20.

55. Logan earned a BA from Williams College before entering the war. See, Kenneth Robert Jankin, *Rayford W. Logan and the Dilemma of the African American Intellectual* (Amherst: The University of Massachusetts Press, 1993), 24–25.

56. John Hope Franklin, "Rayford Whittingham Logan (1897–1982)," *Hispanic American Historical Review* 63 (August 1983): 596–97.

57. Ely Green and Lillian Smith, *Ely: An Autobiography* (Athens, GA: University Press of Georgia, 2004), 238–40.

58. Baldwin, *Chicago's New Negroes*, 8.

59. W.E.B Du Bois, "Returning Soldiers," *The Crisis* 18 (May 1919): 13.

Chapter Two

Frames Refocused

Blinded Black and White Ex-GIs and the Social Re-Orientation of Self in World War Two America

Robert F. Jefferson Jr.

In March of 1946, John Jasper—a *Baltimore Afro-American* reporter—traveled to a site near Avon, Connecticut. The heavily wooded mountainous area and its well-stocked lakes, once the location of one of America's most exclusive boys' preparatory school, now served as the home for one of the army's most ambitious projects: the training of blinded veterans. The occasion that summoned Jasper's appearance was the War Department's shooting of the film *The Social Adjustment Training of the Blinded Soldier* that promoted the training of the soldiers who were assigned to the rehabilitation center. As the newspaper reporter met the GIs undergoing training, he was impressed by the ways in which they negotiated the terrain without canes and other artificial methods and the ways they used touch and sound in order to orient themselves in otherwise unfamiliar areas. But he was equally struck by the ease with which two of the sightless soldiers greeted each other and the businesses they created and developed together. Of the two soldiers, Jasper remarked, "Color has formed no barrier; and the white, the colored, the Japanese-American, and the Indian have trained and worked side by side along lines which each finds to his personal advantage."[1]

The remarks made by John Jasper of the two GIs are of special relevance because they alert us to the ordinariness which the GIs projected under the spotlight's glare and the forces that worked to forge their new identities. The journeys of both of the ex-GIs to the wide screen were atypical, to say the least. The soldier seen working behind the counter was Hilliard Kirby, a white North Carolina resident and former armored force lieutenant with a tank platoon. Kirby was leading his unit during an assault on the Siegfried Line at the Battle of the Bulge in December of 1944 when he was wounded by a grenade fragment, destroying both of his eyes. At that moment, Kirby joined approximately 1,500 soldiers who were blinded while serving in World War II. After being evacuated to a nearby station hospital, the thirty-three-year-old sales engineer spent much of 1945 in several military hospitals before arriving at the Old Farms Convalescent hospital to begin the process of blind rehabilitation.[2]

As he entered the gates of the Connecticut facility, the former sales engineer struggled with feelings of dependency, self-indulgence, and self-pity. His future as a potential wage earner was now in doubt. The GI Bill had just been passed but it was unclear as to what assistance would be available to blinded veterans. Furthermore, prior to his entry into the army, Kirby's attitudes toward African Americans and other minorities were largely derived from the racial prejudices that characterized American society at the time. For example, of the men he encountered in Europe, his reactions to the only African Americans he came into contact with were similar to those described by Larry Nevins in Baynard Kendrick's novel *Lights Out* published during the period, "by their smell or their talk; by the way they acted or the way they thought." At the time, Kirby told one of the hospital staff orientation specialists that he "detested everything about them."

But Kirby's prewar and wartime attitudes toward injury and race were soon tempered by the common experience of blindness and rehabilitation that he held with other sightless contemporaries. Upon arriving at the Avon facility, he, along with several hundred veterans, took classes in a wide array of areas, including Braille, journalism, broadcasting, mathematics, and industrial arts. Kirby was deeply impressed with the orientation instructors, especially Sergeant Archie Lang, a black rehabilitation instructor who had recently been assigned to the center. Under Lang's tutelage, Kirby learned how to travel independently about the hospital grounds, moving first from the bed to the latrine, then from his quarters to the mess hall, to finally being able to travel from the Avon facility to the downtown center of Hartford without an attendant and without a cane. The type of instruction in orientation and mobility that the ex-GI received was consistent with that given to all of the veterans once they arrived at the facility. But the evidence also suggests that Kirby's newly found confidence in "getting around" may have also produced a metamorphosis in his thinking on other issues. Not long afterwards, he was introduced to James W. Hope, a twenty-eight-year-old black sergeant who hailed from Gastonia, North Carolina.[3]

In ways somewhat similar to Kirby, Hope's journey to rehabilitation and his perception of race were profoundly altered by his path to sightlessness. After entering the army in 1942, the former North Carolina Central University graduate was performing field-training exercises with a field artillery unit in Louisiana in August of 1944 when he and several other men found themselves subjected to friendly fire. When the firing ceased, Hope was severely injured with his vision being destroyed in both eyes. While recuperating at Valley Forge General Hospital, he demonstrated considerable cheerfulness and determination, thinking that his condition was only temporary. But after undergoing a series of operations, army doctors told him the possibility of restoring his sight was not possible. As he agonized about his misfortune and future prospects, Hope's self-perception was soon enveloped with new feelings of dread and fear when hospital staff members informed him that he had been reassigned to a new place—Old Farms Convalescent Hospital—in December of 1945. Up to that point, the former sexton had had negative encounters with white servicemen. As he traveled to the Connecticut center, Hope recalled thinking, "I was totally unprepared for what was to happen next because I was removed from the normal world and life I had known since birth—a world where the white man's hate and prejudice was always directed toward the Negro."

The sense of alienation that Hope anticipated in the new setting reached new heights once he arrived at Old Farms. Upon entering the facility, white staff attendants promptly stripped the GI of his long white cane before ushering him into a large room where vocational counselors described the purpose of the hospital. They also discussed the readjustment problems that blinded soldiers encountered at the facility. In the days and weeks that followed, Hope spent a considerable amount of time working with sighted and blind orientation specialists who put him through the paces of obstacle perception and muscular memory. While negotiating the new setting with other blinded army men, he witnessed numerous instances in which racism was simply not tolerated. Among the individuals that left an indelible imprint on Hope's collective memory of that period was Edward Rice—a sightless white sergeant from Massachusetts. Rice, a former Perkins School for the Blind instructor, taught Hope and other soldiers how to walk around the grounds without a guide. But most important, he admonished white and black soldiers who exhibited racial prejudice in the ranks. Years later, Hope described with admiration the young noncommissioned officer's militant pro-normalization and anti-racist message that the young noncommissioned officer imparted to them: "there was a section sergeant in our group who was very popular. He was very intelligent, extremely bright, and totally blind. He would tell us that those who lost their sight in war don't know the meaning of race or prejudice. Blindness blotted out all prejudices. Our aim now is to show the world the things blind people can do." Shortly thereafter, Hope began to develop his own priorities, gradually paving a path to reorientation, taking classes on Braille and typing, economics, and management, where he met Hilliard Kirby.[4]

While somewhat overstated, Kirby's and Hope's initial reactions to their blindness and their somewhat transformed ideas about race are aligned with the observations rendered by Samuel Stouffer and his team of sociologists who studied the behavior of American troops during World War II. In their masterful two-volume study *The American Soldier*, Stouffer and his colleagues inventoried the attitudes of American soldiers on a variety of issues, including their perspectives on disability and race. According to Stouffer, racial friction between black and white soldiers was abated in the army during the Battle of the Bulge in late 1944. Due to a manpower shortage, thousands of black volunteers flooded the ranks to serve in integrated companies fighting at the front. As black and white soldiers stood in the chow lines and engaged in clandestine card games, a rare moment of interracial and interethnic harmony was realized.[5] But overlooked in the analyses of Stouffer and others are the spaces far from the fields of fire where interracial camaraderie took place among black and white GIs and the facilitative roles played by orientation guides like Archie Lang and Edward Rice in the process. It is my contention that as streams of black and white newly blinded soldiers like Hilliard Kirby and James Hope entered the Old Farms facility during the period, touch became sight and they gradually developed a militant pro-independent outlook that was enveloped in an advanced progressive consciousness. And as a result, they became a part of a dynamic environment that encouraged black-white unity and one that offered them an entirely different interpretation of the way the world worked. Blindness, in short, offered them a new framework for understanding the hydra-headed strictures of racism and religious bias in American society. Please bear in mind that these findings are based on archival sources mined at the American Printing House for the Blind in Louisville, the Perkins School for the Blind Archives in Massachusetts, the National Personnel Records Center in Saint Louis, the National Archives and Records Administration, the National Library of Medicine, and the Library of Congress in Washington, D.C., the Hartford *Daily Courant*, issues of the *Outlook for the Blind and the Teachers Forum*, the *BVA Bulletin*, black weeklies, and other unpublished material.

LIGHTS OUT OR BRIGHT VICTORY? THE GIS ENTRY INTO DARKNESS

While the road that brought visually impaired white and black veterans together in Avon, Connecticut, was based on common injury, their initial journey to the rehabilitation center placed them worlds apart. Many of these men came from all walks of life and a variety of backgrounds. Of the 851 blind veterans who entered the Old Farms facility between 1944 and 1947, over 45 percent came from northern and Midwestern states, and approximately 32 percent were originally from states that existed below the Mason and Dixon Line. A much smaller percentage (17 percent) came from Mountain West and Western areas with a smattering of soldiers (7 percent) constituting the remaining portion of the population. More than half of the GIs were in their twenties at the time of their injuries and had attended at least some college before military service. What's more important, most of them came from regions in which relations between blacks and whites followed the Jim Crow pace of Southern life. From drinking fountains and movie houses, to buses and trains, and to schools and churches, the color line ruled the lives of blacks and whites in the region from the cradle to the grave.[6]

But the military experiences of these men were also born, in part, from the army's racial policies during the war. Throughout the 1940s, the American military was rigidly segregated. Blacks could not enlist in the marines or the air corps. The navy permitted them to only serve as mess men. As a result, hundreds to thousands of African Americans were relegated to separate army units commanded by white senior officers and assigned to isolated training facilities that were scattered throughout the American South and the Southwest. When traveling off-post, black soldiers experienced endless bouts of violence and blatant discrimination from hostile white townspeople, not to mention the constant harassment from white military police. What's more, the racial hostility black GIs faced while training in stateside areas followed them once they were deployed to the active theaters of Europe and Asia. Despite numerous examples of distinguished service in combat, African Americans were dogged by racism and vicious rumors of cowardice, fear, and incompetence at almost every turn. "Colored troops do very well under white officers but every time we try to lift them a little beyond where they can go, disaster and confusion follows," Secretary of War Henry Stimson stated at the time.[7]

The numbers of wounded African Americans who suffered permanent sight damage belie the claims made by the Secretary of War, however. Nearly 1,500 veterans lost their sight as a result of service-connected injuries during the Second World War. Of this total, 800 soldiers sustained permanent eye injury while serving during the heat of battle. African Americans constituted approximately 13 percent of this group. What's more, the bulk of the eye wounds suffered by black GIs were sustained during the last two years of the war as the Allied forces withstood long periods of heavy combat while advancing along the battlefronts of the European and Southwest Pacific theaters of operation, especially in the Serchio River Valley of Italy and the jungle areas of the Solomon Islands. As a result, evacuation centers, general hospitals, air evacuation hospital ships, and debarkation hospitals in places like San Francisco, California, Washington, D.C., and Phoenixville, Pennsylvania, witnessed a steady flow of blinded veterans in need of surgical and medical care.

In ways similar to the varied experiences of wounded white and black soldiers, the responses of GIs to their new condition also elicited a wide range of emotions. During their stints in various hospitals leading up to Old Farms, blind GIs generally tended to demonstrate, according to the medical personnel, courage, optimism, and independence, punctuated by moments of depression, anxiety, and resignation. Some may have had the same immediate experience as Russell Williams—an optimistic self-prognosis for partial recovery of vision followed by gradual feelings of uncertainty over permanent sight loss. Enlisting in the army in 1942, Williams was an infantry sergeant who was struck by shell fragments while participating in a fierce battle during the months following the D-Day invasion of 1944. Toward the end of the fighting, the former Indiana high school teacher sustained severe damage to his left shoulder and a traumatic injury to the left side of his face. Of his condition, Williams recalled: "I knew enough about anatomy and physiology to realize that my right eye was completely gone. But I wasn't sure about the left eye. That gave me some hope, but it also dominated my thinking." After drifting in and out of consciousness for four days, Williams spent much of the next year in military hospitals, where he held out hope of saving what little sight remained to him only to arrive at a hospital where he learned some dreadful news. "I was transferred to England, where a doctor realized how preoccupied I was with my left eye and whether I was going to be able to see. He presented the bad news about my left eye in a very honest and supportive way." When asked if he had accepted his loss of sight, Williams recounted, "intellectually I had bought it, but emotionally, I still hung on to the hope that something might be done for my left eye and I held on to that until I reached stateside." After a short stay at Valley Forge Army Hospital in Phoenixville, Pennsylvania, Williams continued to fiercely hold onto those feelings, initially rejecting and then grudgingly accepting the aid of the medical staff before boarding a train heading north to the Connecticut facility in March of 1945.[8]

Old Farms veteran Vasco Hale, an African American resident of West Virginia, held similar thoughts. At the age of twenty-eight in December of 1943, Hale, the highest ranking black officer in a combat engineering battalion of a racially segregated infantry division, was performing maneuvers in California. During a training exercise, he tried to determine why a hand grenade thrown by one of the men in the unit failed to detonate. Realizing the danger and unwilling to risk the lives of the men under his command, Hale moved forward to pick up the defective charge when it exploded in his hand, blinding him in both eyes, causing him to lose his right hand, and four fingers of his left hand, and rendering him partially deaf. At that moment, Hale became one of only a handful of African Americans serving in World War II who were blinded, rendered partially deaf, and bilateral hand amputees as a result of sustaining traumatic injuries. But Hale's wounds were more extensive. Despite receiving nine blood transfusions and enduring lengthy stints in five different military hospitals, medics told him that he would never regain smell or taste. As he began his long road to recovery, Hale publicly exhibited a great deal of cheerfulness, but he privately expressed a great deal of bitterness about the defective charge that caused his accident as well as his prospects for the future. In fact, one of the most difficult challenges that he faced was writing letters to his wife and his parents, informing them of his location and the circumstances that led up to his hospitalization. As a member assigned to the hospital staff remembered the young black officer, "it doesn't appear to me that he has made a good adjustment to his blindness and will probably cause a great deal of difficulty in the future both for civilians and for veterans agencies with his demands. However, he has this justification that he does need a great deal of help and the possibility should be entertained that special funds be set aside for the hiring of an aide to help this patient dress and carry out his daily functions." Stubbornly holding onto his own priorities, Hale was subsequently transferred to a series of medical facilities before arriving at the Old Farms Convalescent facility in 1945.

Even before a sightless veteran arrived at Avon, he discovered that the initial attitudes that he expressed regarding his situation were just the beginning because he still faced the task of resuming the roles he had known prior to the war. As historian David Gerber notes, "the military services discovered what civilian medical practitioners and blind rehabilitation workers had long known: for many blind adults, a period of acute depression, accompanied by feelings of helplessness, follows the loss of vision. At this stage, people may relearn various elementary personal care skills but their rehabilitation focuses mostly on marshaling the psychic resources to face the future with an impairment that is regarded by the average sighted person as one of the most severe disabilities." Upon their arrival at military facilities around the country, servicemen immediately received instruction from medical and civilian personnel on subjects such as personal hygiene, shaving, eating, caring for clothing, Braille, handwriting, taking notes from dictation and reading them back to their instructors, using a rotary phone, and in some cases, opening a pack of cigarettes. And more often than not, the meeting places and schoolrooms of the medical hospitals were staffed by white physicians and counselors, who hailed from every portion of the country and who came from all walks of life.[9]

For many blinded black and white GIs, the integrated military hospitals and the care they received from medical staff and rehabilitation workers marked a new departure in their experiences of injury and hospitalization. It represented the first movement away from a structure in which color, racism, and class antagonism mediated one's place in society. As soon as they entered the facility, the newly arrived patients could not help but notice the non-racial contact among the rehabilitation workers. For example, a veteran rehabilitation officer with the center drew particular praise from incoming soldiers such as Jasper Lollis and officials alike: "Captain Steptoe has been at this hospital for quite some time and while here has demonstrated a versatile ability to influence people no matter who they are and to make friends." Veteran Joseph Hovanos echoed these sentiments. Hovanos entered the Avon facility in 1944 after a German shell exploded near his tank unit during a skirmish in Europe. When asked about the facility years later, the former Ohio steelworker fondly remembered, "the Army and its staff spared no expense or trouble to make black and white soldiers feel at home. Hey, there was a heckuva nice setup over there." Hovanos was also awed by Raymond Frey, who he later described as "one young officer in particular who stood out when I was treated there. He lost his sight while in the army. He helped me to realize that blindness is not too serious an obstacle to my future career, but an inconvenience which has to be overcome by another and which I could master. It was a lesson that I never forgot."[10]

The responses of GIs like Lollis and Hovanos to rehabilitation workers were soon joined by the ambivalent attitudes that the able-bodied population expressed toward them as American servicemen with physical disabilities. Long before V-J Day, the prospect of millions of GIs being suddenly separated from the armed forces and the return of the disabled veterans fueled the energies and imaginations of social workers, psychologists, psychiatrists, sociologists, physicians, fiction writers, and military officials alike. While many celebrated the exploits of the returning GIs, some speculated that the self-absorbed civilians and the public cynicism of postwar America would disillusion servicemen, who had been asked to sacrifice so much during the wartime period. And still others expressed their belief that messages of compassion combined with self-help and self-reliance would greatly facilitate the transition of wounded veterans from the battlefield to the home front. In order to address these concerns, a three-pronged strategy emerged. First, the U.S. government passed omnibus legislation such as the GI Bill of Rights and Public Law 16 to both assist veterans and to reward them for their service. Second, the VA activated a wide array of counseling and training facilities for veterans with service-connected injuries where ex-GIs were to receive vocational and educational counseling to make an adjustment to civilian society. And around the same time, a boom in the publication of advice literature written by psychologists about the plight of returning GIs occurred, and the message of many of these books and articles was specifically aimed at the families of the veterans.[11]

But the problems that black veterans with disabilities would encounter while attempting to adjust to civilian life carried a different meaning. Between 1944 and 1946, black newspapers and journals expressed a great deal of concern about the response of American society to returning black veterans and many predicted that returning African American soldiers would be deeply angered by the unchanged racial climate of the country and would place the onus of their troubled reentry squarely on the shoulders of the federal government, Congress, and the Veterans Administration. To be sure, their words of warning would bear fruit. Black GIs encountered bouts of discrimination when they sought assistance from the VA in their search for better jobs, housing, and educational opportunities. But at the same time, African American disabled GIs were also perceived as objects of unwanted attention within their own respective communities. For example, as prominent African American pundits penned eloquent words to black families, neighborhoods, and communities offering words of self-help and self-reliance and urging their friends, girlfriends, wives, mothers, sisters and brothers, nieces and nephews to exercise compassion and sympathy toward wounded ex-GIs returning to their hometowns, they drew inadvertently upon images associated with people with visible disabilities. For example, a journalist for the *Baltimore Afro-American* stated, "When you greet your wounded friend or relative for the first time, use your intelligence and imagination. Greet him as your friend, who was away and has now returned. Letting horror spread over their features and get in your voice because of his crutches or empty sleeves or sightless eyes will make him realize that you think of him, not as a personality, but as a cripple. Greet the Man, not the wound."[12]

But the more observant among blind black and white ex-GIs quickly came to realize that they were subjected to other pernicious forms of prejudice. Frequently, they experienced being stared at and of being the objects of unwanted attention and unflattering stereotype. More often than not, the attention they received from passersby was not only intrusive but blatant demonstrations of pity intermingled with disdain. For example, upon entering Phoenixville, Pennsylvania, after losing his sight during a combat mission over Vienna in 1944, twenty-three-year-old Lloyd Greenwood remembered, "receiving pats on the head and dollar bills shoved into his pockets from strangers on the street." Claude Lewis, a black enlisted man from Tennessee, recalls that when he arrived in Philadelphia en route to the Old Farms facility that he was sometimes taken as a beggar in search of charity with passengers placing coins in his hands as he departed the train station. And Sergeant Charles Bledsoe distinctly remembers hearing a townsperson make the following comment about blinded servicemen like himself at the time, "I think everything in the world should be done for the blind soldiers, but I don't want to get near them."[13] While these were not the only responses to the blind, they give us a window into the titanic struggles that sightless white and black soldiers faced even before entering the vocational rehabilitation phase of the army's intensive rehabilitation program in Connecticut.

ENTERING A NEW WORLD OF ORIENTATION AND RETRAINING: OLD FARMS CONVALESCENT HOSPITAL AND "FACIAL VISION"

It was this web-like ethos that structured the attitudes of the majority of blind GIs toward social readjustment as they made their way along the twelve-mile road leading up to the Old Farms Convalescent hospital in July and August of 1944. Among these first 200 patients who appeared at the Avon facility were four African American GIs: Fort Adam, Mississippi, resident Jasper Lollis; Bill Blackshere, an infantryman from Hawkinsville, Georgia; Roger Mitchell from New York; and Matthew Parks of Kinston, North Carolina. For Parks, Old Farms would prove epochal (it would be the first of many destinations of rehabilitation as he ventured to Walter Reed General and a VA hospital in Roanoke, Virginia, to undergo multiple operations to repair extensive damage to his legs and arms after the war). Within a few months, the next transport of trainees included Vasco Hale, Richard Brooks, Claude Lewis, Benjamin Peaks, and Thomas Upshaw from Birmingham, Alabama. By the end of 1945, nearly seventy black men had arrived at the military post, anxious to begin the rehabilitation process, preparing them to re-enter civilian life.[14]

The three thousand acres was the home of a former boy's preparatory school, and its core buildings along the Farmington River provided a better than adequate location for the eighteen-week training process that the men would undergo. From the moment the first contingents of disabled soldiers entered the English architecture that dotted the converted school, they stepped into a world unlike any they could hardly have anticipated. First, the atmosphere was devoid of army life and resembled more of a hotel-like setting than a military outpost. And the training process was as intricate and important as any they had previously received. Upon their arrival, the trainees were stripped of the long canes previously distributed to them and taught to use touch to negotiate their immediate surroundings. Shortly afterwards, they were given scale models of the buildings of the hospital which they studied or "brailed" their features before being assigned a sighted escort who worked to familiarize them with the sites on the campus. Training aides then guided blinded soldiers through a site-memory process using a touch method, after which they were presented with a series of mobility problems that took them around the grounds of the facility, first from their rooms to the mess hall, from the classrooms to the Post Exchange, to finally from the training office to the post office.[15]

As they strolled around the grounds, a bond was struck between blinded soldiers and the training aides as they worked to regain the soldier's self-confidence and to restore his physical and psychological equilibrium disrupted by war and sudden blindness. The efforts made by these orientation guides were permanently seared in the memories of the blinded black and white veterans who trained at the facility. For example, Richard Edgecomb, a former infantryman from Florida, witnessed numerous instances of encouragement from black and white orientation specialists at Avon: "William Kusma, a blind orientation guide, is one of the soldiers from whom I have learned hospital travel. He is one of the most valuable instructors here and has proven so over and over again." A New York artilleryman also commented, "I was greatly impressed by the staff led by Alan Blackburn charged with training us in travel. Each of them had been carefully selected for his position in the light of his previous training, aptitudes, and interest. But most of all, they were chosen based on their level of commitment to help us become independent." The talent of black orientation guides like Miles Glynn was also seized upon by ex-soldiers and fellow staff members, alike. For example, during a visit to the hospital, Charles W. Bledsoe, a former instructor for the Maryland School for the Blind and one of the leading figures in the blinded veterans movement, described Glynn to his contemporaries in the following manner: "one of our Negro orientors, is a college graduate and former plumber. Before coming to Old Farms, he worked in a blind man's ward for six years, knows Braille, and is excellent in handling the men." In an interview with Richard Welsh years later, Russell Williams noted, "it seems to me that in using touch and sound, Avon orientation specialists like Alan Blackburn were emphasizing a method of travel that perhaps looked more natural. For them, showing people around and helping them become familiar with their environment was called mobility whereas the primary focus at Valley Forge was on medical and surgical treatments."[16]

One of the orientation and mobility noncommissioned officers who stood out among the Old Farms staff was Archie Samuel Lang. Born in Oklahoma, Lang attended Southern University, where he graduated with a bachelors' degree in history in 1939. But it was in another subject area where he found his true calling. While attending the Louisiana university, Lang worked as a tutor for blind students under the auspices of the Federal Rehabilitation Program. After moving on to continue his studies at Virginia's Hampton Institute, he became interested in studying debilitating eye injuries that were sustained by school-age children and adults, enrolling in numerous graduate courses in Education of the Blind. In 1940, he returned to the Bayou State, where he provided instruction on rehabilitation at the Louisiana School for the Blind before being inducted into the army a year later. But as his desire to work on the Vocational Rehabilitation for Blinded Veterans deepened, his ambition met the harsh realities posed by the Jim Crow policies of the racially segregated army. After being drafted into the army in 1944, he reported to Ellington Field, Texas, where he was assigned to an aviation squadron but he still held hopes of landing a position as a rehabilitation aide in a hospital. However, when he applied to work as a specialist in the War Department's newly created Program for Blinded Soldiers at Valley Forge General Hospital in June of 1944, he was told by the hospital section chief that since they had "so few colored blind at the facility that I do not believe we are justified in taking a colored instructor." However, Lang's fortunes improved dramatically not long afterwards when Colonel Frederick Thorne, the facility's commanding officer and one of the army's chief ophthalmologists, selected him to work as a training aide for the growing numbers of blinded GIs who began to appear at the center. There, he plunged himself into the creative activities staged by the blinded soldiers at the outpost and served as the supervisor of the editorial board for the *Quadrangle Review*. By war's end, Lang's reputation as one of the most highly competent and exquisitely capable specialists in the training division at Old Farms grew to the extent that it traveled beyond Connecticut, ultimately reaching official Washington and landing in the offices of the War Department itself.[17]

But for blinded GIs and staff members at the Avon training facility, Lang's instructional modules of rehabilitation and his individualized attention provided them with a constructive framework for understanding the different frequencies of inequality that they would encounter in the streets, corners, and neighborhoods of the communities that they would re-enter. According to one blinded soldier, "many trainees have taken advantage of what has proved to be a splendid opportunity to take courses in regularly established classes under excellent instructors like Sergeant Lang." And as William Jameson, an officer at the hospital put it, under the tutelage of dedicated orientation aides like Archie Lang, "men are being given the tools with which can be constructed a successful civilian career, and the men—most of them young—are finding, through practical experience, that the plans for the future which they made before the war can be realized and that their futures as useful citizens, as head of families, and as personally well-adjusted human beings, can be assured."[18]

Although somewhat overstated, Jameson's observation points up the distinctive qualities of the Old Farms experience and the degree to which its training differed widely from the orientation and mobility approaches adopted by other rehabilitation centers throughout the country at the time. Outside of the quadrangle, visually impaired white and black veterans stayed abreast of the competing philosophies surrounding the physical rehabilitation of visually impaired GIs within the army's Blind Program. In early 1944, members of the President's Committee on Rehabilitative Measures resolved that the American Blind Program for rehabilitating blind veterans was not meeting the vocational demands of the steady stream of wounded casualties returning from the fronts. But while they agreed that Old Farms was a suitable location for returning service personnel, they found themselves at a quandary in determining which social adjustment training was most appropriate for them. Whereas other rehabilitation hospitals embraced a strict mobility and orientation approach with the soldiers being equipped with long white canes, seeing-eye dogs, and aides to move from room to room, Old Farms instructors advocated spatial techniques based on obstacle perception and muscle memory. Called "facial vision" by hospital psychologist Jacob Levine, orientors instructed blind young soldiers to use obstacle perception to perceive objects at a distance. During a one- to two-month training period, sightless GIs developed the technique to such extent that they were able to walk across Old Farms' village greens, spotting every tree, fire hydrant, hedge, and ash can within reach. "After several months training," Levine exclaimed, "many of them will never run into a wall again."[19]

Some of Levine's colleagues tell another story, however. While "facial vision" was widely publicized in the pages of *Look, Life* magazine, and the *Saturday Evening Post*, the technique was not without its critics. The nature of the Connecticut social adjustment program was at the center of the biting disapproval. For example, Perkins School for the Blind Director Gabriel Farrell noted his displeasure over what he perceived to be "the lack of discipline" among the orientors and trainees while visiting the Old Farms facility at the time, expressing his belief that Avon afforded the blind GIs assigned there little time to reflect on the nature of their injuries and their eventual re-entry into society. "You can't handle human beings for just four months and then wash your hands of them," Farrell complained. But perhaps James Greear, an army ophthalmologist who traveled from Valley Forge to observe the training activities at the hospital may have said it best when he exclaimed, "I observed that the trainees rapidly lose their poise and their posture rapidly deteriorates and the gait becomes that of the typical blind person. Some navigate reasonably well by reflected sounds and the familiar landmarks, while others use the familiar "stumble and crash" method. At this point, my opinion of facial vision reached an all-time low."[20]

It was within the controversy surrounding their rehabilitation, that their growing independence, and an emerging sense of camaraderie gained full expression in March of 1945. Twenty black GIs gathered with eighty other blinded enlisted men and officers at Old Farms and formed the Blinded Veterans Association (BVA). The first of its kind in the country, the association adopted a progressive policy, resolving to improve the life-chances of its membership through self-help, self-mobility, and public support rather than to elicit the feelings of pity and sympathy that the sighted world associated with the civilian blind. But above all, they set high standards for themselves and exhibited a heightened sense of solidarity. For many of the men who entered the association, adjustment to blindness and successful rehabilitation was bound up in dignity-tinged notions of manhood and respectability. For example, many of the BVA members paid careful attention to the message expressed by the association's first executive director, when he uttered the following words in a 1947 editorial published in the association's house organ *The BVA Bulletin*, "since pity is distasteful to us, we should notice upon whom pity falls most often. A ragged helpless-looking beggar is a truly pitiable object. But a well-dressed, capable-looking man is not, though he may be blind. Every white and Negro blinded veteran who makes a good adjustment to blindness is showing a sizable number of people what they need to know about the blind." These words of aggressive normalization also informed their outlook on the existing prejudices that divided Americans in the wider society. For example, unlike the larger veterans' organizations such as the Disabled American Veterans, the BVA and its leaders condemned racism and anti-Semitism, and advocated integrated chapters at the national, regional, state, and local levels. More importantly, they also actively supported civil rights initiatives to advance the cause of African American equality throughout the 1950s and 1960s.[21]

Among the leaders present who embodied the spirit of interracial normalization were William Hasse, Herald Smith, and Vasco Hale. As some of the first sightless GIs who entered Old Farms as editors of the *Quadrangle Review*—the post newspaper—they aggressively pushed the BVA message of self-independence and interracialism throughout the issues of the *Quadrangle Review*. In the first editorial statement, they pronounced: "discrimination is a part of the business of being blind. But other groups share our problem and all suffer the effect of prejudiced thinking. We have to avoid that way of thinking." Together, each GI rose to leadership positions in the early years of the BVA throughout the late 1940s, the 1950s, and the 1960s. But Hale was so deeply moved by the events at Old Farms and the high standards set by the BVA that he became the organization's national secretary in 1951 (the first African American to be elected in such capacity during the period) and would hold public office in the association for the next fifteen years. He would also continue his bonds with the BVA long after leaving the position, traveling every year to the annual meetings and marching on foot with his comrades to the cheers of hundreds of onlookers during its annual parades. And as Hale's work with the BVA grew, so did his interest in issues of disability and race. Around the same time, the former mathematics and biology teacher stated his intentions to pursue a graduate degree in vocational rehabilitation in order to provide guidance to blinded black and white veterans like himself. "I hope I can prove myself adequate to hold the position of vocational guidance counselor so that I can be helpful to the physically handicapped," he told his Avon contemporaries. He later settled in nearby Hartford, Connecticut, where he rose to the presidency of the city branch of the National Association for the Advancement of Colored People in 1953. Hale's activities in the BVA and his movement into a career relating to rehabilitation and racial equality are significant because they demonstrate how disability offered the ex-GI a new framework for understanding the fight for equality in American society.[22]

The visually impaired black and white ex-GIs at Old Farms had barely been organized for an entire year when they were confronted with an incident that would vividly remind them of the issues of race, disability, and social power that awaited them. In February of 1946, twenty-seven-year-old Isaac Woodard boarded a bus in Georgia heading home to New York. Still in uniform, he had much for which to be grateful. He had just returned to the states after surviving enemy fire in New Guinea and the Philippines with the 429th Port Battalion for which he was awarded a Good Conduct Medal and a Battle Star that went along nicely with his honorable discharge. However, the war for Woodward was just beginning. After stopping a short distance beyond the Georgia–South Carolina border, he promptly got into an argument with the bus driver who refused to wait while he used the restroom. After the bus arrived in nearby Batesburg, South Carolina, the skirmish between the two men escalated to deadly proportion when the driver called upon local police to arrest Woodard for creating a "disturbance on the bus." When the beleaguered soldier struggled to defend himself, several officers proceeded to beat him unconscious before using a nightstick to gouge his eyes out, severely damaging his corneas and permanently blinding him in the process.[23]

In the days and months that followed, the BVA, along with the NAACP and the United Negro and Allied Veterans Association, rallied to support Woodard by sponsoring his rehabilitation program when he entered Old Farms and holding fund-raising activities and benefit shows to aid his return to the Bronx a year later. But activists in the Blind Veterans Association saw the decorated veteran through a prism that was molded by their own common experience and a fierce determination to be independent. Reflecting on the public's racial attitudes regarding Woodard and other blind black veterans, Lloyd H. Greenwood, the BVA executive director, stated, "it's a stupid idea for people of a community to assume the attitude that a blind veteran is social undesirable, for it relegates him to a life as an outcast and embitters him to feel that more than his eyesight is gone."[24]

But perhaps the issues of rehabilitation and race gained their fullest expression in May of 1946 when over 100 blinded war veterans reassembled at Old Farms to discuss a matter of vital importance to them—the release of Baynard Kendrick's novel *Lights Out* and its characterization of social relations that existed among the visually impaired black and white veterans who attended the rehabilitation center during the wartime period. Voicing their dismay with the author's portrayal of the state of race relations at the facility, rank-and-file black and white GIs resolved in overwhelming numbers to condemn the book, forcing Kendrick to resign from his position as honorary chairman of the BVA's Board of Directors. The movement taken by the BVA's members was significant because Baynard Kendrick was an active participant in the rehabilitation movement at the outpost during the war.

Throughout the 1950s, Kendrick's novel and its depiction of race relations among black and white World War II GIs continued to be the subject of future discussion among BVA members, both white and black alike. In 1951, Kendrick's story of blinded World War II veterans moved from screen play to the wide screen as a major motion picture film. Among those who continued to register their discontent over its portrayal of sightless soldiers were ex-GIs like Hilliard Kirby and James Hope, GIs who came from racist and class-bound areas but were now united through injury to the fight to build a movement to forge a new world in which sightlessness is a part of the normalizing process.[25]

CONCLUSION: SITES UNSEEN REVISITED

With the opening of Hines Hospital in Illinois, Old Farms Hospital closed its doors in 1947. As the civil rights struggles of the 1950s and 1960s gave way to the movements toward the individualism and austerity of the last decades of the twentieth century, the public memory of the interracial independence that the facility promoted faded into obscurity. On November 11, 2009, more than four hundred students, former employees, volunteers, media, and townspeople assembled at Old Farms Convalescent Hospital to commemorate the sixty-fifth anniversary of the opening of the facility. Speeches were made by members of the Avon Historical Society and the VFW members about the soldiers who entered its gates as callow youth and who were introduced to sightlessness during the war-torn years of the 1940s.

How much the spectators knew about the way the legacy of interracialism that the hospital helped to create among its patients during the war and its immediate aftermath is difficult to determine. Indeed, as the spectators clapped their hands paying tribute to the post's memory, they probably knew next to nothing about the lessons of social learning embraced by the soldiers who frequented its corridors. But for one particular soldier, the facility held special resonance. As one of the BVA's early leaders and the VA's first Chief of Blind Rehabilitation at Hines Hospital, Russell Williams told his personal story to the audience and expressed his belief that Old Farms was a reframing experience that led many to think in ways that they had not considered before the war. "Each blinded soldier was free to question his beliefs and choice of interest. It was this thinking that enabled him to live as a full human being free from prejudice and discrimination. I made a lot of good friendships with those fellows," he claimed. Perhaps, little did Williams realize it at the time, but the atmosphere that he described to the Avon audience that day is but one chapter of a larger work that needs to be written about the American experience with war, disability, and race in the twentieth century. The wider implications of his remarks are yet to be realized.[26]

NOTES

1. John Jasper, "Prejudice Can't Live Where Men Can't See," *Baltimore Afro-American* (March 9, 1946), 5.
2. *Social Adjustment Training for the Blinded Soldier*, directed by U.S. Army (Washington, DC: War Department, 1946, Video, 2009); Irvin P. Schloss, "BVA Convention Seeks Strong VA Program," *The New Outlook for the Blind* 45 (October 1951): 233.
3. *Social Adjustment Training for the Blinded Soldier*; "Bulletin Board," *BVA Bulletin* 2:6 (June 1947): 6. Rehabilitation instructors like Archie Lang came to Old Farms with a wealth of education, training, and experience working with visually impaired adults before entering military service. For more recent studies on the army's blind rehabilitation programs and its orientation program, see Steven Miyagawa, *Journey to Excellence: Development of the Military and VA Blind Rehabilitation Program in the 20th Century* (Lakeville, MN: Galde Press, 1999); Caroline Bradford, "Army Rehabilitation at Old Farms Convalescent Hospital," *Military Medicine* 182 (January–February 2017): 1454–55.
4. Ibid.; John Jasper, "Prejudice Can't Live Where Men Can't See: Blind Vets at Old Farms Learn Man-Sized Jobs," *Baltimore Afro-American* (March 9, 1946), 5; Letter, C. A. Pfeffer to Dr. Gabriel Farrell, April 13, 1946, Folder 230: Correspondence with Avon Old Farms Convalescent Hospital, Dr. Gabriel Farrell Collection, Perkins School for the Blind Archives, Samuel P. Hayes Research Library, Watertown, MA.
5. Samuel Stouffer, et al., *The American Soldier, vol. 2: Combat and Its Aftermath* (Princeton: Princeton University Press, 1949).
6. The methodology that supported this study involved several venues. Data was culled from the following sources: Milton D. Graham, et al., *851 Blinded Veterans: A Success Story* (New York: American Foundation for the Blind, 1968); Home Addresses of Patients in Blind Rehabilitation, Old Farms Convalescent Hospital, Avon, Connecticut, Charles W. Bledsoe Papers, Charles Warren Bledsoe Orientation and Mobility Archives, Museum of the American Printing House for the Blind, Louisville, KY. I then cross-checked the names of these individuals against the National Archives' Access to Archival Databases (AAD) located at the url address https://aad.archives.gov/aad/series-list.jsp?cat=WR26.
7. For more on the black military experience in World War II, see Gail Buckley, *American Patriots: The Story of Blacks in the Military from the Revolution to Desert Storm* (New York: Random House, 2001); Bernard C. Nalty, *Strength for the Fight: A History of Black Americans in the Military* (New York: New Press, 1986); Jack D. Foner, *Blacks and the Military in American History* (New York: Praeger, 1974); Ulysses G. Lee, *United States Army in World War II, Special Studies: The Employment of Negro Troops* (Washington, DC: Office of the Chief of Military History, 1966); Henry L. Stimson Diary, September 27, 1940, Henry L. Stimson Papers, Yale University Library.
8. Richard L. Welsh, "Inventing Orientation and Mobility Techniques and Teaching Methods: A Conversation with Russell Williams," *RE:view* 37:1 (Spring 2005): 2–6.
9. David A. Gerber, "In Search of Al Schmid: War Hero, Blinded Veteran, Everyman," in David T. Mitchell and Sharon L. Snyder, eds., *The Body and Physical Difference: Discourses of Disability* (Ann Arbor: University of Michigan Press, 1997), 116; History of Blind Program, Charles Warren Bledsoe Manuscript Collection, Chronological Files, Box: 06, 1910–June 1946, American Printing House for the Blind, Louisville, KY; William A. Jameson Jr., Post History: Old Farms Convalescent Hospital (SP), Avon, Connecticut, undated, RG 112, Records of the Office of the Surgeon General, Box 1, Old Farms Convalescent Hospital, Folders: Orders, Memos, History (1944–1947), NARA II, College Park, MD.
10. Profile Outline of Jasper Lollis, August 14, 1944, RG 112, Records of the Office of the Surgeon General, Folder: OPHTH-Zone of Interior, Old Farms Convalescent Hospital-Profile Outlines-July 31–November 1944, NARA II, College Park, MD; Letter, R. E. Hoover to Dr. Gabriel Farrell, August 3, 1945, Folder 246: Correspondence, Dr. Gabriel Farrell Collection, Perkins School for the Blind Archives, Samuel P. Hayes Research Library, Watertown, MA; Profile of Joseph M. Hovanos, July 31, 1944, RG 112, Records of the Office of the Surgeon General, Folder: OPHTH-Zone of Interior, Old Farms Convalescent Hospital-Profile Outlines-July 31–November 1944, NARA II, College Park, MD.

11. For works that advocated such points of view about returning World War II veterans, see Betty Barton, *When the Disabled G.I. Comes Home* (New York: D. Appleton-Century Company, 1944); Edna Yost and Dr. Lillian M Gilbreth, *Normal Lives for the Disabled* (New York: MacMillan Company, 1944); Willard Waller, *The Veteran Comes Back* (New York: Dryden Press, 1944); Dixon Wecter, *When Johnny Comes Marching Home* (Boston, MA: Houghton Mifflin Co., 1944); George K. Pratt, *Soldier to Civilian: Problems of Readjustment* (New York: McGraw-Hill Book Company, Inc., 1944); Irvin L. Child, Marjorie Van de Water, et al., *Psychology for the Returning Serviceman* (Washington, DC: Infantry Journal and Penguin Books, 1944); Charles Bolte, *The New Veteran* (New York: Penguin Books, 1946); Roy R. Grinker and John T. Spiegel, *Men Under Stress* (Philadelphia, PA: The Blackiston Company, 1945); Herbert Kupper, *Back to Life: The Emotional Readjustment of Our Veterans* (New York: L. B. Fischer, 1945); Edward A. Strecker and Kenneth E. Appel, *Psychiatry in Modern Warfare* (New York: MacMillan Company, 1945); Alanson H. Edgerton, *Readjustment or Revolution* (New York: McGraw-Hill, 1946); Robert A. Nisbet, "The Coming Problem of Assimilation," *American Journal of Sociology* 50:4 (January 1945): 261.

12. Harold Wilke, "Greet the Man Returning Home, Not the Wound; Tips for Welcoming the Wounded," *Baltimore Afro-American* (January 20, 1945), 5. For a more extensive discussion on the African American response to returning black veterans after World War II, see George W. Franklin, "An Evaluation of Counseling and Employment Activities of Disabled Negro Veterans," (PhD diss., Purdue University, 1955), 2–6; Robert F. Jefferson, "Enabled Courage: Race, Disability, and Black World War II Veterans in Postwar America," *The Historian* 65:5 (Fall 2003); Jennifer E. Brooks, *Defining the Peace: World War II Veterans, Race, and the Remaking of Southern Political Tradition* (Chapel Hill: University of North Carolina Press, 2004).

13. Baynard Kendrick with Kathern F. Gruber, "The Birth and Development of the Blinded Veterans Association," 43, Baynard Kendrick Papers, Special Collections, University of South Florida, Tampa, FL; Letter, Charles W. Bledsoe to Dr. Gabriel Farrell, December 14, 1944, Folder 246: Correspondence, Dr. Gabriel Farrell Collection, Perkins School for the Blind Archives, Samuel P. Hayes Research Library, Watertown, MA.

14. Home Addresses of Patients in Blind Rehabilitation, Old Farms Convalescent Hospital, Avon, Connecticut, Charles W. Bledsoe Papers, Charles Warren Bledsoe Orientation and Mobility Archives, Museum of the American Printing House for the Blind, Louisville, KY; Insert: List of Blinded Casualties, Letter, M. E. Randolph to Dr. Charles Griffith, undated, RG 112, Records of the Office of the Surgeon General, Box 1357, Entry 31, HD: 730, Folder: Blinded Casualties, NARA II, College Park, MD.

15. John Boyd Coates, et al., *Medical Department, United States Army: Surgery in World War II: Ophthalmology and Otolaryngology* (Washington, DC: Office of the Surgeon General, Department of the Army, 1957), 193–207; Frederick Woltman, "Army Hospital Pioneers New Techniques for Orienting Blind Vets to Useful Life," *New York World-Telegram* (February 14, 1945); Caroline Bradford, "Army Rehabilitation at Old Farms Convalescent Hospital," *Military Medicine* 182 (January–February 2017): 1454–55.

16. Letter, Charles W. Bledsoe to Dr. Covalt, April 14, 1946, Box: 06, 1910–June 1946, Folder: April–June 1946, Charles Warren Bledsoe Manuscript Collection, Chronological Files, American Printing House for the Blind, Louisville, KY; Richard L. Welsh, "Inventing Orientation and Mobility Techniques and Teaching Methods: A Conversation with Russell Williams *RE:view* 37:1 (Spring 2005): 8–16.

17. Memorandum, Archie S. Lang for the Commanding Officer, 79th Aviation Squadron, April 25, 1944, Subject: Qualifications of EM, Letter, J. N. Greear, Jr. to Major M. E. Randolph, June 24, 1944, all in RG 112, Records of the Office of the Surgeon General, Box 1357, Entry 31, HD: 730, Folder OPHTH-ZI-Old Farms Convalescent Hospital, Personal Information, Applications, etc., 1944, 1945, 1946, NARA II, College Park, MD; World War II Army Enlistment Records, Access to Archival Databases (AAD), Archives.gov, NARA accessed August 2, 2017; Archie Samuel Lang Draft Registration Card, Serial Number 2224, Order Number 1515, 1940–1947, *The National Archives at Fort Worth, Texas, USA; Louisiana, First Registration Draft Cards, compiled 1940–1945*; Record Group 147, Records of the Selective Service System, 1926–1975, Ancestry.com. accessed August 2, 2017; *Quadrangle Review* 3:2

(May 30, 1945): 2, RG 112, Records of the Office of the Surgeon General, Box 1357, Entry 31, HD: 730, Folder OPHTH-ZI-Old Farms Convalescent Hospital, *Quadrangle Review,* NARA II, College Park, MD; Archie S. Lang in the US, Find a Grave Index, 1600s-Current url: http://www.findagrave.com/cgi-... [database on-line], Provo, UT, USA: Ancestry.com accessed August 2, 2017.

18. *Quadrangle Review* 3:2 (May 30, 1945): 1; William A. Jameson, Jr., "Old Farms Convalescent Hospital Where Blinded Soldiers 'Come Back,'" *Outlook for the Blind and the Teachers Forum* 38:10 (December 1944): 271.

19. Coates, *Surgery in World War II*, 159–160, 188–189; William Jameson, "Post History: Old Farms Convalescent Hospital," RG 112, NA; Jacob Levine and Alan R. Blackburn, "Rehabilitation of the Newly Blinded," *Journal of Clinical Psychology* 2:2 (1946): 140–45; David K. Boynick, "Blinded Soldiers Learning to See Through 'Sound Perception,'" Mattoon, Illinois *Journal Gazette* (December 7, 1944): 1; Frederick Woltman, "Miracle of Facial Vision Gives 'Sight' to the Blind," *Pittsburgh Press* (February 28, 1945), 21; Frederick Woltman, "Blind Veterans Learn to Be Self-Reliant," *Pittsburgh Press* (March 2, 1945), 25.

20. "War Blind Soldiers Learn to Live Again at Old Farms Convalescent Hospital in Avon, Connecticut," *Look* 26 (November 27, 1945), 31–33; "Army Blind School," *Life* 21:20 (November 11, 1946), 101–4; Arline Britton Boucher and John Leo Tehan, "They Can 'See' Without Eyes," *Saturday Evening Post* 217:43 (1945), 26; Gabriel Farrell, "Blinded Casualties of the Army: A Review of Programs and Proposals," August 1945; Letter, Dr. Gabriel Farrell to Alan Blackburn, undated, Folder 231: Correspondence, Avon Old Farms Convalescent Hospital, Dr. Gabriel Farrell Collection, Perkins School for the Blind Archives, Samuel P. Hayes Research Library, Watertown, MA; Memorandum, Major Elliott Randolph for General Rankin, November 18, 1944, RG 112, NARA; Letter, Gabriel Farrell to Robert B. Irwin, November 2, 1944, Folder 246: Correspondence, Perkins School for the Blind Archives.

21. Minutes, Organizational Meeting of the Blinded Veterans Association, March 28, 1945, Folder: January–March, 1945, Charles Warren Bledsoe Manuscript Collection, Chronological Files, Box: 1910–June 1945, American Printing House for the Blind, Louisville, KY; Editorial, "Seeing is Believing," *The B.V.A. Bulletin* 2:3 (March 1947): 2.

22. *Quadrangle Review* 3:1 (May 16, 1945), Folder: Valley Forge, Miscellaneous, 1940s–1950s, Warren Bledsoe Orientation and Mobility Archives, American Printing House for the Blind, Louisville, KY; "1947 Election Nominees: Vasco Hale," *BVA Bulletin* (July 1947); "BVA Convention Seeks Strong VA Program," *The New Outlook for the Blind* (October 1951), 233; Letter, Vasco Hale to John W. Davis, September 23, 1948, John W. Davis Papers, Drain-Jordan Library Archives, West Virginia State University, WV; Gerold J. Demeusky, "Disabled Veteran Who Lost Eyes, Hand in Blast Now Learning to Help Others," *Hartford Daily Courant* (no date), 20.

23. Isaac Woodard, "Sworn Testimony for Civil Lawsuit," November 1947, NAACP 1940–1955 Legal File, Isaac Woodard, 1943–1950, NAACP Papers, pt. 8 (Discrimination in the Criminal Justice System, 1910–1955), Series B (Legal Department and Central Office Records, 1940–1955), Reel 30.

24. "Blinded Vets Group Raps Discrimination," *Lubbock Evening Journal* (August 6, 1946), 2.

25. Baynard Kendrick with Kathern F. Gruber, "The Birth and Development of the Blinded Veterans Association," Baynard Kendrick Papers; Ray Frey, BVA Bulletin, Message from the President, Charles Warren Bledsoe Manuscript Collection, American Printing House for the Blind.

26. Russell Williams-Terri Wilson, "Avon Commemoration to Honor BVA Pioneers," *BVA Bulletin* (Summer 2009). http://www.bva.org/sum09bulletin/avon.html (accessed October 9, 2013).

Chapter Three

Have Gun, Will Travel

The Deacons for Defense and Justice, Armed Self Defense and the Long Black Power Movement

Selika M. Ducksworth-Lawton

The Deacons for Defense and Justice (DDJ), a veterans' militia in Jonesboro and Bogalusa, Louisiana, illustrated the interweaving of nonviolence and armed self-defense, and highlighted the especially important role of veterans in leading local movements. Examining why they chose armed self-defense over nonviolence illustrates how Louisiana veterans' visions of manhood and republicanism intersected with their military experiences to shape how activists forced the state of Louisiana to enforce the 1964 Civil Rights Act.

The Deacons for Defense and Justice picked up their guns and protected the African and white Congress of Racial Equality activists who used the courts to enforce the Act. The Deacons basically enforced the Civil Rights Act themselves in Louisiana from 1965 to 1967. Operating in the cities of Jonesboro and Bogalusa in Louisiana, the Deacons used long guns to protect CORE and local Bogalusa Voters League activists from the Original Knights of the Ku Klux Klan (OK-KKK). Members of the OK-KKK infiltrated the police force in those cities. These police officers allowed the OK-KKK to break the law in front of their faces. They refused to arrest the violent Klan members, to investigate, or to intervene to stop beatings carried out right in front of them. These police officers would not protect African American rights to integration. The 1880s Supreme Court decision *Cruikshank* encouraged these officers to ignore their obligation to protect African American rights. The Deacons' guns changed that equation. The Deacons posed a difficult question to the Original Knights: will you die for white supremacy? The answer was no. This utilization of guns, combined with cameras and the press, forced the state and the federal government to act. The Deacons forced Louisiana police officers to intervene and arrest violent Klansmen. Louisiana is the only Southern state to integrate without the use of federal troops. The Deacons created space and safety for the civil rights activists to dissent without being killed.

AZ Young, Second World War veteran and Louisiana Deacons' leader, noted:

> It was early in 1965 when the Bogalusa Voters League was in its struggle for freedom and we found out the Klan's was bringing pressure upon the Negroes and the Negro community. They were night riding, there were Negro women and children being caught on the street, brutalized and beaten and what have you. We felt that the city police did not protect us and give us we felt we was entitled to. We felt the only means to counterattacking this was to form an organization by the name of the Deacons, a protective agency, to protect the Negroes in their homes and in their community.[1]

Local histories illustrated the interweaving of armed resistance with nonviolence in rural and small towns. African American veterans' leadership in the civil rights movement sparked armed resistance movements as well as nonviolent movements. Their influence came from the concepts of politics of protection, concepts of small-r republicanism (special responsibilities and leadership roles from military service), and concepts of masculinity. The armed resistance organizations, which protected nonviolent protesters, buttressed the nonviolent movement. Student Non-Violent Coordinating Committee (SNCC) leader Cleveland Sellers described what the Deacons in Louisiana did and why SNCC valued them.

> They were in fact armed and their responsibility was to make sure that the march was safe. If they could eliminate an aggressive action or eliminate sharpshooters or people taking advantage of the march [Freedom From Fear March, 1965] then that's what they would do . . . They would tell us certain things we needed to know along the way. They would go into the wooded areas. They would check cars out. They would keep their eyes on all of these things, but the spirit was around self-defense.[2]

The Deacons in Bogalusa grew out of grassroots Congress of Racial Equality (CORE) activism in Louisiana from 1963 to 1966. "On or around July 29, 1963, Louisiana CORE [Congress on Racial Equality] Field Secretary Ronnie M. Moore brought into Louisiana many task force workers. The primary purpose for their arrival was to start a VEP [voter education program] program in some of the roughest areas of the state. In the very beginning they concentrated most of their efforts on the 6th Congressional District; however, later they expanded to the 5th Congressional District to work only on VEP.

All of the direct action took place in the parishes of the 6th Congressional District."[3]

These VEPs became the grounding for the Summer Projects. Under the direction of Dave Dennis, the Southern Program Director for the Southern Regional Office (SRO) of CORE, headquartered in New Orleans (and who was also directing the Congress of Confederated Organization's projects), the CORE Summer Projects in Louisiana through Florida focused on integration, voter education and registration, economic access through building coops, and extending services to African American communities throughout the southeastern United States. The most famous of these was Freedom Summer in Mississippi, but the Summer Project in Louisiana, while less famous, was just as influential. Their local use of direct action, and their responses to the violence of Mississippi and Louisiana, directly affected the Deacons and SNCC.

The Summer Projects identified communities with existing organizations for in-depth, targeted organizing. CORE preferred to see an organized activist apparatus in the area already, rather than build from the ground up. A 1964 report rejected St. Tammany Parish, just across the lake from New Orleans, because of a lack of organization and leaders. CORE chose West Feliciana, Jonesboro, Bogalusa, East Baton Rouge based on scouting reports and recommendations from the SRO (Southern Regional Office) staff.[4] The Jonesboro and Bogalusa activism grew out of joint projects between the CORE SRO staff and the local activists. SNCC cooperated with CORE and continued the practice of overlapping staff and cooperation with CORE in Louisiana as well.

"The main thrust of SNCC's program at present is voter registration in rural areas . . . "[5] SNCC decided that helping in these areas, which were the hardest to organize but had the largest numbers of unregistered African Americans, was vitally important to enforcing the 1965 Voting Rights Act and 1964 Civil Rights Act. By organizing these areas, SNCC activists reasoned that they could open the door to educational awakening. CORE valued integration more for its long-range plans, but SNCC's registration plans made sense in the short term to CORE, which allowed for collaboration. Both SNCC and CORE believed that these efforts would create a more egalitarian society.[6]

SNCC, like CORE, also understood that mere nonviolence would not lead to a utopia. Both focused on power and education as vital parts of long-range agendas.[7] They believed that working with local activists, who presumably knew the needs of the community, and creating local solutions, would support sustainable action. The Summer Projects were meant to be exemplars of this idea.[8]

The Deacons for Defense and Justice were not the only protective agency that emerged during the era of mass protest. In June 1964, black military veterans formed a similar organization in Tuscaloosa, Alabama . . . Joseph Mallsham, a Korean War veteran and labor organizer at Tuscaloosa's Zeigler meatpacking plant, was one of several older activists who sought to convince the angry hotheads of the futility of violent disorders. Rather than burn down the town, he argued, blacks ought to organize their own protective agency to prevent violent incidents like the one at the church that day and to protect the movement against the Ku Klux Klan. "If we're going to do this," Mallsham told them, "let's do it right."[9]

Ernest Sims, Fitzpatrick, Robert Hicks, Gail Jenkins, and AZ Young, the leaders of the Deacons and the group they protected, the Bogalusa Voters League, were bound by ties of military experience and family. These leaders were enlisted U.S. Army veterans, or in Jenkins' case, married to one. Their influence came from a specific locality of ideals, experiences, and geography. The Deacons created space for nonviolent protestors to speak and act in an environment dominated by corrupted state officials and security forces from 1965 to 1968. The Deacons created the ability for nonviolent protesters to enforce the Civil Rights Act of 1965. Enforcement was key. The Deacons provided local support for enforcement.

African-American military service during World War II and Korea had an impact. Southern veterans who returned home after serving the cause of freedom were reluctant to acquiesce to inferiority. The action taken by President Harry Truman in ordering the desegregation of the armed services in 1948 provided additional momentum. Thereafter, southern African-Americans served in the military with the express understanding that racial equality rather than segregation was the official policy of the United States armed services. Many local-level Civil Rights activists in the 1960s were military veterans.[10]

Cleveland Sellers of the Southern Christian Leadership Conference (SCLC) described the Deacons in the eyes of the mainstream movement.

The Deacons for Defense was a group whose responsibility was to defend their communities or themselves against attack. It was never a group of retaliation. We involved them [in the March Against Fear] to protect the marchers. They were in fact armed, and their responsibility was to make sure that the march was safe. If they could eliminate an aggressive action or eliminate sharpshooters or people taking advantage of the march [Meredith was in the hospital from being shot from behind a bush on the first day of the march] then that's what they would do. We tried to learn from them. They would tell us certain things we needed to know along the way. They would go into the wooded areas. They would check cars out. They would keep their eyes on all of these things, but the spirit was around self-defense. This was something emerging inside the movement.[11]

Historians have given the Deacons and the Bogalusa Voters League limited attention. Right now there is one work on the overall Deacons movement: Lance Edward Hill's *The Deacons for Defense: Armed Resistance and the Civil Rights Movement* (2004). It claims that the Deacons and their leadership were working-class radicals. The class analysis misses the fact that the men and women did not see themselveds as radicals, and actually rejected anything that smacked of radicalism or communism. These were very capitalist, patriotic, moderate people. Hill's work does not cover the military and veterans' aspects of the Deacons' work, and barely covers the Bogalusa to Baton Rouge march. Hill places the Deacons within a wider context of armed struggle, contrasting them with the Panthers, et al. He also includes interviews with Ernest Thomas, the leader of the Jonesboro Deacons. His analysis of success and failure is within the movement and he does not address in any way the issue of veterans' influence in organizing or directing the tactics of the Deacons. Hill does not analyze the tactics themselves, either.

Peniel Joseph's *Waiting Til the Midnight Hour* (2006) and Patrick Jones' *The Selma of the North* also make the point that nonviolence and armed self-defense have a complicated, contradictory, foundational relationship. Jones writes that "nonviolence and armed self-defense often worked 'in tension and in tandem' throughout the modern African American freedom struggle. Yet, this complexity has been submerged under the more popular and less controversial narrative of nonviolent direct action."[12] Armed resistance and nonviolence are both opposed to each other and interlocking in each other. Without guns, nonviolent activists historically were either killed quietly or deterred. Without the attention of nonviolence through media management, armed resistance could be numerically overcome by corrupt use of state power and dismantled.[13]

L. LaSimba M. Gray Jr.'s *The Deacons for Defense and Justice: Defenders of the African American Community in Bogalusa, Louisiana during the 1960s* (Winter Park, FL: Four-G Publishers, 2000) is a quasifictional account of the Deacons, blending interviews with fiction and Christian ideology to place the Deacons as Christians warriors. Adam Fairclough's *Race and Democracy: The Civil Rights Struggle in Louisiana, 1915–1972* (Athens: University of Georgia Press, 1995) summarizes the Deacons, and gives a general list of their involvement. Fairclough tends to downplay the Deacons' contributions, attributing the success in Bogalusa to the Bogalusa Voters League, the Deacons' sister organization (an NAACP-derived organization).[14] CORE member Peter Ian Honigsberg's memoir, *Crossing Border Street—A Civil Rights Memoir* (2000) gives the view of an outsider in Bogalusa, facing the Klan terror as a special target: a white man, a Yankee, a "race traitor." This made him more of a target and gave him more access to the Deacons. Deacons protected white CORE members who were "special" targets for Louisiana's Original Knights of the Ku Klux Klan (OK-KKK). His testimony is supported by media accounts and interviews with Miriam Feingold, in 1965–1967 taped interviews with several members of the Bogalusa movement, including Hicks, Burris, and Jenkins. Robert F. Williams' *Negroes With Guns* also references the Deacons and the Bogalusa movement. Greta de Jong discusses the special role that CORE played in working with rural local movments and empowering local peoples in her work, *A Diffferent Day: African American Struggles for Justice in Rural Louisiana, 1900–1970*.

Historians like John Dittmer, Emilye Crosby, Peniel Joseph, and Charlie Cobb challenge the concepts of when Black Power emerged, whose voices mattered, and how local movements were critical to enforcement. These new historiographical interpretations, called the long Black Power movements, posits that Black Power includes armed self-defense and emerged long before the 1966 Meredith March. It placed armed resistance within the Black Power movement. Hill posited that historians ignored armed resistance for many years because it did not fit the narrative of nonviolence preferred by civil rights historians.

> According to conventional wisdom, nonviolence provided the impetus for change during the civil rights movement. In some quarters it has become heresy to suggest otherwise. Historians, for the most part, continue to labor under this truism. But the experience of the Deacons . . . stubbornly contradicts the myth of nonviolence. Nonviolence as the motive force for change became a reassuring myth of American moral redemption . . . that racial segregation and discrimination were handily overcome by orderly, polite protest and a generous American conscience, and that the pluralistic system for resolving conflicts between competing interests had prevailed. The system had worked, and the nation was redeemed. I was a comforting but vacant fiction . . . In the end, segregation yielded to force as much as it did to moral suasion.[15]

Emilye Crosby's groundbreaking *Civil Rights from the Ground Up: Local Struggles, A National Movement* (2011) joins John Dittmer's *Local People: The Struggle for Civil Rights in Mississippi*, to ground the ideas of armed self-defense within the Long Civil Rights movement and the Long Black Power movement. Crosby sees armed self-defense as an extension of Black Power (indeed, so did Kirkpatrick of the Deacons), while Dittmer sees armed self-defense as proto Black Power and something more complicated. He details ad hoc self-defense in Mississippi. Dittmer's work intersects with Charles Cobb's *This Nonviolent Stuff Will Get You Killed: How Guns Made the Civil Rights Movement Possible* (Basic Books, 2014) and Akinyele Omowale Umoja's *We Will Shoot Back: Armed Resistance in the Mississippi Freedom Movement* (2013) to describe how rural organizing in many ways demanded the presence of armed self-defense for survival. Crosby's work includes interrogations of the politics of protection and the special place that veterans held in the civil rights movement, as protectors but also of respect and leadership. Crosby also discusses in the "politics of protection article" how veterans were special targets of supremacist abuse. The idea of veterans as special targets because of their leadership and military training is supported in Douglas Bristol Jr. and Heather Marie Stur's *Integrating the US Military: Race, Gender, and Sexual Orientation Since World War II* (2017). Several chapters detail abuse and targeting of veterans and active-duty military personnel by civilian and police supremacists in the U.S. South. Yet, Joshua Bloom's *Black Against Empire* argued that the Black Power movement viewed African American segregated spaces as reservations, occupied spaces due to colonialism, and set the Black Power movement into an international anti-colonialist framework, sets armed self-defense as a precursor, necessary but not sufficient, to Black Power; a more conservative cousin. This author posits armed self-defense as the bridge between nonviolence and Black Power; the presence of armed self-defense married with local republicanism explains why the Deacons saw themselves and their people as Americans, and saw access to American rights as their primary focus. Black Power's questioning of capitalism and the assumption of capitalist interplay with democracy was explicitly rejected by the Deacons in their dealings with Revolutionary Armed Movement (RAM).

The Deacons' conservative mission manifested itself in two very distinct ways. The first manifestation of conservatism was the Deacons' refusal to become involved with leftist-radical communist organizations. Despite early hysterical FBI descriptions of the group as "militant"[16] the Deacons were committed to a very conservative, rural vision of capitalist republican democracy; small "r" republicanism. Just as their charter argued, they wanted their rights under the Constitution. They did not want to change the capitalistic democracy; they simply wanted access to its benefits, like security in their own homes. Because the Deacons were mainly veterans, they felt that they had earned the rights. FBI agents shared this African American variation on classical republicanism.

> Black republicanism represents an amended version of classical republicanism . . . black veterans expressed appreciation for the institution of citizenship, using republican rhetoric to define good citizenship by emphasizing its duties and obligations . . . for veterans also emphasize the importance of citizens' rights—anathema to classical republicanism—which they perceive to be a necessary counter to white domination, their domination by an internal enemy. Black republicanism . . . incorporated some of the tenants associated with black liberalism, particularly radical egalitarianism. Both are committed to making America realize its democratic promise. But the two-part company in key areas—first among them their attitudes toward the state. Black republicans . . . are less willing to countenance state intervention than radical egalitarians . . . Perhaps more importantly, masculinity is a point of departure between the two ideologies. Black republicanism, like its mainstream counterpart [clas-

sical republicanism—italics mine] is gendered; radical egalitarianism, in theory if not in practice, is not.[17]

Christopher S. Parker's *Fighting for Democracy: Black Veterans and the Struggle Against White Supremacy in the Postwar South* documents veterans' ideals of republicanism and activism. Timothy Tyson's *Radio Free Dixie: Robert Williams and the Roots of Black Power* (1999) and Robert Williams' *Negroes With Guns* (1962, reprint 1998) both posit armed self-defense within rural traditions. They also discuss the way white supremacists of that time abused government and governmental institutions to harass and legally lynch activists asking merely for Constitutional rights. Andrew H. Myers' *Black, White and Olive Drab: Racial Integration at Fort Jackson, South Carolina, and the Civil Rights Movement* discusses African American soldier activism in the 1940s and how African American soldiers worked with civilians to create a de facto integration environment and to limit segregationists' ability to abuse governmental functions to harass African Americans. Michael Cullen Green's *Black Yanks in the Pacific: Race in the Making of American Military Empire after World War II* builds on the idea that military service imparts ideals, skills, and values that spill over into activism at home.

ENTER THE DEACONS

Ernest Thomas and F. D. Kirkpatrick from Jonesboro, Louisiana, spoke in Bogalusa at an exploratory meeting on creating a militia on February 21, 1965. That same night, February 21, CORE's Bill Yates, Steve Miller, Fenton, and two Deacons road in one car. African American Bogalusa native and future Deacon Royan Burris was behind them, to protect Yates, Miller, and Fenton on their way back to New Orleans. They were tailed by a car full of whites. A Corvette forced Burris off the road and threatened him. Shaken, the group continued. Robert Hicks announced publicly that the Bogalusa Deacons were in business at the February 22nd Mass meeting.[18]

The popular male coach at the African American high school, Coach F. D. Kirkpatrick, quietly supported the Deacons. This support led to his firing in March. Over the week of March 24th, the firing led to sit-ins and clashes. The FBI was already monitoring the Deacons at Jonesboro and Bogalusa. This caused the FBI to intensify its monitoring. Through March 1965, Washington Parish Sheriff Jesse Cutrer stalled implementing any of CORE's demands and ignored the Bogalusa Voters League (BVL).

In response to Cutrer's stalling tactics, on April 4th, BVL and CORE activists began picketing downtown stores to force integration. They combined the pickets with voter registration drives. Students from Kansas State University arrived to help with the voter registration drives. This set off the

OK-KKK, and they came out en masse. They chased and beat students and activists alike.[19] On April 7th, three whites tried to grab Bill Yates as he left Robert Hicks' house in the morning. He escaped the would-be kidnappers. The same night, approximately sixty OK-KKK members marched and left two coffins, one with Yates' name on it, outside the union hall where the BVL and CORE were running voter registration drives with the help of the students from Kansas State University.[20]

James Farmer, the national president of CORE, arrived in Bogalusa on April 8th. Bogalusa police turned back four hundred African American students who attempted to march on City Hall. Police actions led to high racial tensions. That morning, Kansas State University students attempted to canvass for voters. OK-KKK members chased students in four cars.[21] On April 9th, James Farmer and Ronnie Moore led five hundred marchers from the union hall to City Hall. Farmer was attacked twice even though the march was supposed to be protected by the one hundred police there. Instead, the OK-KKK darted in and out of the crowd to hit people in front of the watching police without the Bogalusa police attempting to stop them. The OK-KKK went after reporters and photographers; even an FBI agent was attacked without police intervention. Six hours later, on their second attempt, the marchers arrived at City Hall. Sheriff Cutrer met them on the steps, arguing that differences could be negotiated. The BVL did not believe him, even as they accepted the offer of negotiation.[22]

The national news media reported the violence, and the ineffectiveness of the police. The news reports placed intense pressure on governmental officials to negotiate an appropriate settlement. With Selma fresh on people's minds, and the Voting Rights Act stinging in white supremacists' imaginations, both sides were intransigent. The supremacists were aggrieved because they felt that their birthright of discrimination was being taken from them, and this time by popular will. They could not continue to rail against the Supreme Court, as they had with *Brown*. The United States Congress, in two short years, passed two laws striking at the heart of disenfranchisement and segregation—the 1964 Civil Rights Act and the 1965 Voting Rights Act. This was democracy, and they were not going to accept it without a fight.

Vice President George McGovern warned Louisiana Governor John Julian McKeithen that the growing crisis needed to be addressed. Cutrer still refused to meet with the BVL for weeks. He justified his stalling by creating in April a puppet African American organization, the United Civic League, filled with a set of handpicked conservative separationist blacks, to sit in the negotiations from the Farmer March. The BVL countered by threatening another march and embarrassing all the governmental officials involved by accusing them of bad faith. Governor McKeithen refused to recognize the United Civic League and forced real negotiations by the end of April.[23] "Thus, to eventually control the country, the insurgent must control the people ... the support of the people is a measure of the insurgents' ability to control the people, whether through their willing cooperation or as a result of threats, acts of terrorism, or the physical occupation of their community."[24] A large group of segregationists supported the OK-KKK in using violence against both African Americans and whites who called for law and order. "While time, access to the people, and guerilla warfare are the tools the insurgent uses to build a successful strategic structure, two essential elements make up the foundation of the structure: a cause around which to rally popular support and a weak governmental administrative and law enforcement apparatus..."[25] These Klansmen whipped whites who were not "separate" enough, bombed the front office of a newspaper that condemned them, and would physically intermingle with neutral whites in Bogalusa, emerging to try to attack, then blending in again. "Inefficient police methods and the absence of effective administrative control allow the insurgent cadre the freedom of movement necessary to recruit new followers. The absence of a well-run police force also provides fertile ground for the employment of terror by the insurgents against those individuals who persist in supporting the government."[26]

In Bogalusa, as in other areas of the South, sympathizers riddled the security forces. The 5th District Federal Court of Appeals, in response to a lawsuit filed by a Deacon/BVL, placed the Bogalusa police and state patrol under consent decree twice in 1965 and 1966 to create training and implementation plans to prevent violence to African Americans and whites integrating public facilities. On multiple occasions the police ignored illegal mob behavior in front of them, aided it, or protected the OK-KKK. In May of 1965, the OK-KKK drove through the African American section of Bogalusa, throwing out pamphlets threatening death to CORE workers and telling African Americans to throw CORE out of town. The illegal parade was headed by the police chief's car, with him in it.[27] One of the two African American police officers was shot, and no one was tried for the murder, while the suspect paraded around and boasted openly of his crime. Lawlessness was open and nationally known in Bogalusa in 1965.

> In an insurgency, the way to destroy the insurgent is to attack him at the source of his strength: the population. If the counterinsurgent forces can minimize insurgent access to the population, the insurgent's access to manpower, supplies, and intelligence will be curtailed.... The intelligence information that the insurgents derive through their ability to inspire or intimidate the people also provides a key link in the chain of factors that enable the guerillas to survive and prosper... If denied the ability to move quickly and easily among the population, the insurgent will become... like a fish out of water... [28]

Enlisted service taught the leadership skills to fight insurgents utilizing terror. The Deacons applied concepts that they learned in the U.S. Army to fighting the Klan in Louisiana. Basic enlisted service in the army taught Sims, Young, Hicks, Thomas, Burris, and other leaders to emphasize using appropriate weapons. Standardizing weapons allowed the stockpiling of ammunition and weapons, in the same way that the U.S. Army uses standardized weapons to allow for ease in fixing, maintaining, and buying ammunition. Standardizing to commonly available military surplus also made it easier to acquire weapons and have enough for them to be readily available . . . again, a lesson from military service.

Basic army training emphasized patrolling, communications, technology, and discipline in the World War II and Korean conflict era. Special extended training in 1942 also taught illiterate soldiers to read and write. African American troops benefitted from this.[29] The U.S. Army screened enlistees for literacy, discipline, health, etc.[30] Emphasizing individual responsibility on top of army basics was a hallmark of World War II and Korean conflict training. Army training in World War II benefitted from experiences in World War I, the Philippines, the Mexican border, and the Spanish-American war. This led to training that emphasized patrol, interception, communications, and discipline.[31]

Patrolling, communications, operational secrecy, intercepting intelligence by using walkie-talkies, following orders, and firepower discipline within rules were skills the U.S. Army taught enlisted as a part of basic training, and reinforced through periodic practice.[32] The Deacons applied these skills to protecting civil rights activists. Military service itself predisposed veterans to armed self-defense and serving in the Deacons.

HOW DOES THE ARMY TEACH THESE CONCEPTS?

In many ways, the Deacons functioned as an Intelligence and Reconnaissance platoon (I & R platoon), or as a rifle platoon. "During this period every tactical infantry formation, from platoon through division, included a reconnaissance and surveillance organization. Each infantry company had two trained scouts in every twenty-rifle platoon. Every infantry battalion had a small trained reconnaissance section, directed by the battalion intelligence officer (S-2). Each infantry regiment included a small I&R platoon, specifically trained and dedicated to answering the reconnaissance and intelligence needs of the infantry regiment's commander. This platoon was assigned to the headquarters company of the infantry regiment, charged with the following mission: The principle mission of the regimental intelligence platoon is to serve as the special intelligence agency of the regimental commander, for the collection, recording, evaluation and dissemination of information, under the supervision of the regimental intelligence officer (S-2). The platoon is also charged with counterintelligence measures and surveillance . . ."[33] Sims,

Hicks, and Young all emphasize the patrolling, communication, interception, intelligence gathering, operational secrecy, and deception that are hallmarks of I&R platoons in World War II and Korea. Rifle platoons emphasize patrolling, discipline, and use of communications technology that the Deacons applied to their environment.

The idea of portable radios and communications came directly from Intelligence and Reconnaissance and Rifle platoons (I&RR platoons). Soldiers saw portable radios (walkie-talkies) in use, and used them, in World War II and Korea. Korea, in particular, had a problem with ambushes, which made walkie-talkies particularly important. Walkie-talkies were also used to call in air strikes and communicate with headquarters during both the Second World War and Korean conflict.

The DDJ used citizen band radios, (CBs), army surplus portable radios, and police scanners to facilitate communication and to deploy interceptors. They also used army-style patrols to gather intelligence, to discourage night riding and sniping, to deter assassination and intimidation attempts using cars, and as a reconnaissance-style (forward observer) warning system to warn of mass Klan incursions. The reconnaissance patrols were military inspired. They were familiar to veterans of the Korean conflict, who used them to warn of North Korean and Chinese incursions. CORE and the OK-KKK believed the patrols to be effective. These patrols discouraged casual Klan violence, and made local African Americans feel safer. The communications, in combination with the patrols, allowed them to identify OK-KKK members' cars and confront them. The communication combination also allowed them to more easily escort CORE workers from Bogalusa to New Orleans, some fifty miles away (the interstate did not directly link the two cities). One example of this was the protection of Bill Yates of CORE by the DDJ as he left Hicks' house on April 7, 1965. Three whites in a car attempted to kidnap him. The communication system allowed the driver to call for help, and the intervention of DDJ activists allowed Yates to escape.

Charles Sims' media interviews illustrate how the Deacons applied U.S. Army training to fighting Klansmen. Sims, a working-class small-business owner and worker at Crown Zellerback Paper Mill who led the Jonesboro Deacons and was the acting spokesman for the Louisiana chapters, discussed weapons during an interview. He argued that, "A shotgun is for close-range stuff. I don't intend to let a man get close enough to me to hit me with a shotgun. [Interviewer: So you prefer a rifle?] The best they make."[34] Thomas also recommended rifles and handguns, usually .38 caliber revolvers.[35] Revolvers were cheap and reliable, two important considerations for an impoverished group struggling against economic retaliation. Semi-automatics were very expensive in the 1964–1966 period. The media spread rumors that Deacons had automatic weapons, .50 caliber and .30 caliber, and grenades, etc., and were stockpiling more. Sims and Thomas claimed .30 carbines were present in the organization. Sims and Thomas undertook a national tour in the summer of 1965 to raise money for arms and to seed new DDJ chapters. This led to FBI and media speculation about the extent of their firepower, speculation encouraged by the DDJ. During the March Against Fear, Thomas told an interviewer on camera (an interview which appeared on the ABC Nightly News) that the Deacons had .50 carbines.[36] Other white and African American activists echoed the claim. The FBI, after much wasted investigation in response to segregationist hysteria and the media claims, claimed that the DDJ had no such firepower, and had only shotguns, .38s, and .45s.[37]

Miriam Feingold, in her interviews for the Wisconsin Historical Society, asked AZ Young about Deacons' activities and opinion of gun rights. Young responded:

> We usually have a continuous patrol around Negro neighborhood in order to keep nightriders from coming in, destroying homes or picking out one particular person in a family, taking them off and killing them, hanging them, whatever their position might be. So we, they are not an offensive organization, this is a defensive organization.
> I don't think there's a law for nobody to carry a gun on them as an individual, but we do have a law in the state of Louisiana that a person can carry a gun on the seat of their car for the protection of themselves and the peoples who are accompany them. There was at one time, Governor McKeithen, during the time of our struggle, issued an order to state troopers to pick up all guns in the Bogalusa area and we naturally bucked against this request of the governor because we firmly believed that this was only a trick to take the guns from the Negroes and disarm us and leave the Ku Klux Klan with their guns and leave us in a terrible predicament.[38]

Another army influence on the DDJ was the use of communications equipment to facilitate defense. The DDJ used citizen band radios, (CBs), walkie-talkies, and police scanners to facilitate communication and to deploy interceptors. Sims noted that "We have telephones, naturally, word of mouth, and we have some powerful walkie-talkies. We can receive a lot of different calls on the walkie-talkies that we can't transmit, but we can receive them. And that's what bugs the white man today. We was intercepting their calls. . . . The Ku Klux Klan, sometimes the police calls . . . "[39] Sims then described intercepting a call about a doctor being intimidated in Covington, around twenty-eight miles away. He got there in seventeen minutes, picked up the doctor, intervened when three white men tried to stop the doctor, and drove the doctor back to Bogalusa. Sims said that the Deacons had "pretty fast automobiles. They're a little faster than the usual car."[40] The FBI and others believed these patrols were highly effective, within and outside of the organization. The patrols discouraged casual Klan violence, and made local African Americans feel safer.

Deacons expressed a preference for experienced military veterans on multiple occasions. The Deacons "only admitted men over the age of twenty-one . . . Several had served in World War Two and the Korean War."[41] Earnest Thomas, one of the leaders of the Jonesboro unit, was a Korean War veteran.[42] Charles Sims was an army veteran, as was Percy Bradford Lee (head of the Bogalusa Unit), Robert Hicks, and most of the members in the leadership of the BVL and the DDJ.[43] Hicks entered the army in 1947. Sims was drafted into WWI, and Young was a World War II veteran. Robert Hicks, a former first sergeant whom the group elected to leadership, worked with Charles Sims of the Jonesboro Deacons to create Deacons with military discipline and skill. Both men explicitly cited military service and tactics like patrolling and communication and fire discipline as important.

The Deacons understood the importance of being clearly perceived as protectors, and not as vigilantes. The act of incorporating, the emphasis on the Second Amendment, the internal disciplining of members, the refusal to allow "showing off," all led to a reputation for seriousness, which allowed the Jonesboro and Bogalusa chapters to face down armed Klan opponents on several occasions. Whites tried to portray them as criminals or vigilantes. By 1965, the FBI determined that the real criminals were the OK-KKK, and, in June–August of 1965, the courts agreed.[44] The discipline of the DDJ allowed the whites in the FBI and the judge on the case to focus on the conduct of the OK-KKK and the security forces in Washington Parish (the Parish Bogalusa was in), not on the conduct of the DDJ. While the FBI viewed the Deacons with some concern, one factor limited the FBI's concern: mounting violence in other places. Selma, Montgomery, in February of 1965, and other incidents in Milwaukee that year helped to force the FBI to spread their attention. The actions of the ultra-segregationist whites and police in Bogalusa also limited FBI sympathy. The unruly ultra-segregationists during one march on April 9th beat an FBI agent, among others, without any attempt at controlling the violence by the Bogalusa police.[45] The OK-KKK continued to aim indiscriminately at unknown whites and included FBI agents as victims. This helped to limit FBI sympathy for the group.

Deacons also deliberately spoke to the FBI agents themselves. "Speaking off the record to local agents, Deacons readily admitted that they deliberately inflated their numbers and weapons for the purpose of deterring the Klan."[46] Another source noted "_____ stated that there were between 250 and 300 members of DDJ with the parish; he said that they did not carry arms, altho possession of shotguns and rifles for hunting is common place in the area." A Bureau memo on July 17th from W. C. Sullivan to F. J. Baumgardner discussed the exaggeration, pointing out that most people in Louisiana, African American or white, were pretty heavily armed, and that the Deacons steered clear of suspicious partners. This, for the time, was an evenhanded assessment. The FBI, ironically, believed the Deacons. A second Deacon also talked to an FBI agent, and asserted self-defense as the only interest.

> On March 24th, 1965____ was contacted and interviewed regarding another matter. ____ voluntarily furnished information that he is a member of Deacons of Defense and Justice, Inc. (DDJ). Jonesboro, which he described as a civic organization dedicated to civic improvement in the Negro community and to protection of the civil rights of persons in the Negro community. ___stated that the DDJ is entirely non-violent, but that some of the members have firearms for self-defense with the Ku Kluc Klan' who might go to the Negro section of town to engage in violence. There was observed a double barrel shotgun, a single barrel shotgun, a .30 caliber rifle and a .22 caliber rifle all standing in the corner of the office ... The .30 caliber rifle was observed to have the name . . . tared on it. During the conversation with ___ it was observed that ____walked into the office, and handed him a loaded .45 caliber revolver in a leather holster from a desk drawer ... _____Stated that members of the DDJ do not engage in armed patrols, but that the stories of their armed patrols were given out to discourage klansmen and persons of that kind from going into the Negro section to cause trouble. He stated that there have been a number of crosses burned in the Negro section within the last year or two. And that one night in July 1964, a motorcade of about 30 cars with persons wearing hoods and whites robes drove through the Negro section of town, led by a police car of the Jonesboro Police Department.[47]

The Deacons preserved operational secrecy for several reasons. This first reason was safety. Secrecy kept members from being harassed by the Klan-infiltrated police force. This secrecy protected DDJ members from police brutality and false arrest. Secrecy also prevented members of the OK-KKK from assassinating Deacons at will. The secrecy also made the OK-KKK pause; the Klansmen never knew when or where the Deacons would appear, so they could not prepare ambushes or defend very well against the paramilitarily organized group. Secrecy, then, gave operational surprise to the Deacons. It allowed them to surreptitiously gather intelligence on OK-KKK members and their infiltration of the Bogalusa police, to find out when Klan attacks would happen, and to use unconventional tactics to deter against the Klan and defend against armed attacks. The operational secrecy of the Deacons also made them appear stronger, and more frightening than they were. They claimed between fifty to fifty-five chapters of uncertain strength. Sims and Thomas shrewdly manipulated the news media, by claiming thousands of members, upsetting segregationists and undermining gradualists' arguments for slowing or not enforcing integration. The secrecy led some to speculate that the group was preparing for a coming race war, a possibility the FBI found alarming.

The army also influenced DDJ discipline. The DDJ presented itself as a well-disciplined, professional group, both in terms of internal discipline and fire discipline. This made them seem more dangerous in the eyes of whites. They patrolled, stockpiled weapons, gave interviews, and emphasized a clear, very limited set of conservative aims that few, including King, could criticize.[48] "Hot heads" or undisciplined people in their manner would not be tolerated.[49] The fire discipline and marksmanship led to the Deacons never killing anyone, even though they deliberately discharged weapons to break up threatening mobs (at the Cassidy Park incident and the May 8, 1965, march; the defense of the Burris Barbershop/BVL march May 29, 1965), and to prevent violence several times.

In Bogalusa, weapons seemed natural and were essential in everyday life. Louisiana in the Korean conflict had the highest number of enlistee casualties for African Americans, and some of the lowest age of enlistments. With Fort Leroy Johnson, and several military facilities within easy driving distance, Louisiana had a number of veterans in the area. These veterans, who knew the terrain, were familiar with .30 06 shotguns, .45 revolvers, and military discipline. The geography of these areas did not frighten them. These geographies, with the predominance of pine trees close to the two-lane rural highways, hills in the north and swamps in Hancock, large amounts of Spanish moss interspersed with deciduous trees, created dark shadows and low visibility. This landscape provided veterans with places to set observers and watch for Klan nightriders. They could also draw back into the dense landscape to melt away from attackers. Supremacist violent attacks tended to be ambush or sniper attacks on small groups in cars, or open attacks in open small-town areas (the street, Cassidy Park, Highway 190) with impunity and surety that the supremacists would not be arrested. The openness of the latter geographies made them amenable to photographers and videographers videotaping the brazenness of the violence. The ambush attacks in the rural, unincorporated areas were far more difficult and dangerous to deal with.

The need for partners and walkie-talkies made sense in this environment. If a car followed them, other cars with armed guards could easily join the chase and scare off the ambusher. Houses along the way could set snipers, warn drivers of ambushes and snipers, or provide diversion. Calling the local authorities was not an option in Tunica or Washington, because the local security forces were riddled with Klansmen. In Washington Parish, Sherriff Jesse Cutrer's car was rumored to have led one Klan night ride through unincorporated Bogalusa in February of 1965. His collaboration with the OK-KKK led to state and federal sanctions and the lawsuit by Hicks, which forced the security forces of Louisiana to provide protection for the Deacons or allow them to do so.

MILITARY AND MANHOOD

In interviews with black Korean conflict veterans, one theme emerges consistently: responsibility. Some men believed the military taught them individual responsibility and to "be men." The army explicitly taught individual responsibility.[50] Examples include supporting family members: "So I was just supporting . . . while I was there I was helping support the family and when I left, you know, I just sent money back home. I didn't need it, you know, I had enough . . . I didn't have a lifestyle before I left . . ."[51] Other veterans interviewed for this author's dissertation also argued that the military had helped teach them about manhood and moved them to civil rights organizing. "I later became a member of the NAACP . . . While I was in the military, I joined the NAACP. I was considered to be a kind of a militant by some people's standards, because when I saw something that was wrong, I tried to do something about it, even if it wasn't directly, and I was good at writing letters. And I still do that today. I did . . ."[52] Another man argued, "Oh yes, definitely. [*This had shown you were competent.*] Right, to withstand this and stay in the army. It don't have to happen to you all the time for you to have deep feelings about it. You can have someone close to you, some people you know, you hurt just as bad. The bleeding don't stop; just doesn't with me. This is my thoughts on things."[53] These men had fairly conservative views on manhood, as competent, confident, responsible, and assertive. Several joined the NAACP.

A similar view of manhood, but perhaps even more conservative, was held by Deacons and by African American men in Bogalusa and Jonesboro.

> But some racist practices were intolerable insults to black manhood . . . Compromising the sanctity of the family was one of those transgressions . . . violence against the family and home violated the ancient right to a safe hearth and home. "When they saw their own children get hit or beaten," recalls Patterson, the men, "reacted very differently." Non-violence obliged black men to stand idly by as their children and wives were mercilessly beaten, debasement most black men would not tolerate. They clung tenaciously to their fragile claims to manhood and honor. It should surprise no one that non-violence ultimately discouraged black men from participating in the Civil Rights movement in the South . . . Black men, unlike their crusading saviors, understood that there was no equality without honor. CORE began to slowly grasp the dilemma they had created for black men.[54]

The view of manhood as assertive, strong, protective, and honorable was both a military and civilian mainstream one. In a period with the draft, where many men had military service, this view was widespread. It was very, very popular. It underlay the Deacons' very existence. Charles Sims, head of the Deacons in Bogalusa in 1965, described it as " . . . the Southern white man is almost like Hitler in the South. He been dictating to the Negro people, 'Boy, this,' and 'Uncle, that' and 'Granma, go here," and the people's been jumpin'. So, he gets up one morning and discovers that 'Boy,' was a man, and that he can walk up and say something to 'Boy' and 'Boy' don't like what he say, he tell him to eat himself—you know? And then if he blow up, there's a good fight right there."[55] The idea of manhood here is very important. The Deacons call themselves men in a very deliberate manner. White supremacist men saw African American men acting within American masculine norms as scary. Supremacists particularly singled out African American veterans for the enforcement of submissive behavior through violence and lynching. The military influence shows through in the assertiveness of these men. It is different than the mere honor cultures of the South. The precision of the organization, the separation of roles, the fire discipline, contrasted sharply with the ad hoc nature of Klan violence and the undisciplined nature of the violence utilized by state and local forces against the movement.[56]

The Deacons in Bogalusa and Jonesboro saw their mission as to protect the African American community from Klan violence and intimidation. Sims articulates this several times. In the *National Guardian*, when Sims is asked if his group is really a police unit, he claims, ". . . I would say a defense guard unit."[57] He continues in the same interview to point out that, ". . . the local, the federal, the state, everybody objects to us carrying weapons . . . but we had to arm ourselves because we got tired of the women, the children being harassed by the white nightriders."[58] The *Wall Street Journal* echoes this claim, "The armed groups claim their only purpose is to protect the Negro community from violence by an increasingly hostile—and also armed—Klan now resurgent in many areas of the rural South."[59] The article goes on to quote one unnamed leader, "'if the Klan tries to hit us, they will get hit back.' . . . There could be 'hitting back' for many a town this summer, for the armed groups are growing rapidly."[60] In *Ebony* magazine, the author notes that ". . . unrestrained by local police, Bogalusa whites have embarked on a campaign of organized terror unparalleled in Louisiana history . . ."[61] *Newsweek* called the Deacons, "a guns for the Negroes vigilante group born in racial crises in Jonesboro and Bogalusa to defend black communities against marauding white terrorists . . ."[62]

One unnamed informant in the FBI file claimed that "the Deacons was [sic] founded to give Negroes protection in the community . . . see that no churches or homes were bombed or burned."[63] Rowan Burris of the Bogalusa DDJ described the mission of the DDJ in 1966.

> The Deacons had started approximately two years ago when the movement first began in Bogalusa. We found the Klansmen were their strongest hope here in Bogalusa and we knew that we would have quite a few obstacles against them that would confront us. Therefore we had to organize ourselves

as men to get together to protect Civil Rights workers as they came into our city.[64]

Veterans were important to the civil rights movement in several ways. As local catalysts, they occupied a special space in the nonviolence, armed resistance, integration, and Black Power. Some, like Korean conflict veteran Ivory Perry, were organic intellectuals. "Organic intellectuals direct the ideas and aspirations of their class even though they hold no formal status or employment as 'intellectuals.' Social action constitutes the indispensable core of their activity. Organic intellectuals not only analyze and interpret the world, they originate and circulate their ideas through social contestation." They act, and in doing so make space for others to act.[65] Others were more traditional local organizers, drawing on military experience, labor-organizing experience, and geographic knowledge to create their opportunities. The Deacons for Defense and Justice illustrated the importance of veterans to local organizing. They used skills honed in WWII and Korea to provide safe spaces for local nonviolent protest. Military experience could not be separated from their local labor-organizing experience. The threads interact.

NOTES

1. Wisconsin State Historical Society, Miriam Feingold Collection. Interview with AZ Young by Miriam Feingold. 1966. Transcribed by author.
2. Henry Hampton and Steven Fayer, *Voices of Freedom: An Oral History of the Civil Rights Movement from the 1950s through the 1980s* (New York: Bantam Books, 1990), 286.
3. Wisconsin State Historical Society, Miriam Feingold Collection, reel 2, slide 389, Report. CORE's Direct Action in Louisiana.
4. Wisconsin Historical Society CORE Collection, SRO, Box 1, folder 6, St. Tammany Scouting report BSC 93-4, Bogalusa Scouting report BSC 101.
5. Wisconsin State Historical Society, Miriam Feingold Collection, Reel 1, no. 207 SNCC report 3.
6. Wisconsin State Historical Society, Miriam Feingold Collection, Reel 1, no. 207 SNCC report 3.
7. Wisconsin State Historical Society, Miriam Feingold Collection, Reel 1, no. 207 SNCC report 3-5.
8. Wisconsin State Historical Society, Miriam Feingold Collection, Reel 1, no. 207 SNCC report 3-7.
9. Simon Wendt, "The Roots of Black Power? Armed Resistance and the Radicalization of the Civil Rights Movement," in Peniel E. Joseph, ed., *The Black Power Movement: Rethinking the Civil Rights–Black Power Era* (New York: Routledge, 2006), 150-51.
10. *Papers of the Southern Christian Leadership Conference*, 1954-1970 Part 4: Records of the Program Department, Introduction Copyright © 1995 by University Publications of America, accessed May 16, 2006, at http://www.lexisnexis.com/academic/guides/african_american/sclc/sclc4.asp.
11. Henry Hampton and Steve Fayer, *Voices of Freedom: An Oral History of the Civil Rights Movement from the 1950s through the 1980s* (New York: Bantam Books, 1990), 286.
12. Patrick D. Jones, *The Selma of the North* (Cambridge: Harvard University Press, 2009), 123.
13. See the Arkansas Race Riot in the 1930s and Robert Williams in North Carolina in 1958 for examples.

14. Adam Fairclough, *Race and Democracy: The Civil Rights Struggle in Louisiana, 1915–1972* (Athens: University of Georgia Press, 1995), 378, 380.

15. Lance Edward Hill, *The Deacons for Defense: Armed Resistance and the Civil Rights Movement* (Chapel Hill: University of North Carolina Press, 2004), 258–61.

16. State Historical Society of Wisconsin CORE SRO Box 1, *Memo to Director*, from SAC, Los Angeles, 9/29/65, 2.

17. Christopher S. Parker, *Fighting for Democracy: Black Veterans and the Struggle Against White Supremacy in the Postwar South* (Princeton: Princeton University Press, 2009), 199–200.

18. State Historical Society of Wisconsin CORE SRO Box 1, File 4, *Summary Report Bogalusa Incidents* pp. 1–2. State Historical Society of Wisconsin CORE SRO Box 1, File 4, Summary of Jonesboro Incidents pp. 1–3.

19. Adam Fairclough, *Race and Democracy: The Civil Rights Struggle in Louisiana* (Athens: University of Georgia, 1999), 362.

20. *US v Original Knights of Ku Klux Klan*, Civ. A. No. 15793 250 F Supp. 330 1965 United States of America, by Nicholas deB. Katzenbach, Attorney General of the United States, Plaintiff, v. Original Knights of the Ku Klux Klan et al., Defendants. United States District Court E.D. Louisiana, New Orleans Division, December 1, 1965. http://www.leagle.com/decision/1965580250FSupp330_1513/UNITED%20STATES%20v.%20ORIGINAL%20KNIGHTS%20OF%20KU%20KLUX%20KLAN.

21. Adam Fairclough, *Race and Democracy: The Civil Rights Struggle in Louisiana* (Athens: University of Georgia, 1999), 362.

22. *US v Original Knights of Ku Klux Klan*.

23. Ibid.

24. Andrew Krepinevich, *The Army in Vietnam* (Baltimore, MD: Johns Hopkins University Press, 1986), 9.

25. Ibid., 10.

26. Ibid., 10.

27. *US v Original Knights of Ku Klux Klan*.

28. Andrew Krepinevich, *The Army in Vietnam* (Baltimore: John Hopkins University Press, 1986), 11.

29. Ulysses Lee, *The Employment of Negro Troops. U.S. Army in World War II, Special Studies* (Washington, DC: Center of Military History, U.S. Army, 1990), 250–55.

30. Ibid., 258–59.

31. Roger Spickelmier, MAJ, USA, *Training of the American Soldier During World War I and World War II* (MA Thesis, U.S. Army Command and General Staff College, 1987), 19–20, 51, 52, 56, 93–102, 104–5, http://www.dtic.mil/dtic/tr/fulltext/u2/a185226.pdf, accessed July 26, 2017.

32. Ken Chamberlain, "What was Army Training Like During World War II?" *Army Times*, March 24, 2018. Historical video of training film, https://www.armytimes.com/news/your-army/2018/03/24/what-was-army-basic-training-like-during-world-war-ii/, accessed July 26, 2018.

33. MAJOR RICHARD J. RUNDE, JR., U.S. Army, *The Intelligence And Reconnaissance Platoon, 1935–1965: Lost In Time*, A thesis presented to the Faculty of the U.S. Army Command and General Staff College in partial fulfillment of the requirements for the degree MASTER OF MILITARY ART AND SCIENCE, Fort Leavenworth, Kansas 1994, 20–21 file:///C:/Users/selik/Desktop/i%20and%20R%20Platoons.pdf.

34. "Armed Defense," an Interview with Charles R. Sims, in Jay David and Elaine Crane (ed), *The Black Soldier: From the American Revolution to Vietnam* (New York: William & Morrow, Co., 1971), 194.

35. Roy Reed, "Armed Dixie Negro League is Spreading," *Des Moines Register*, Sunday, June 6, 1965, 8-G.

36. Henry Hampton (producer) Eyes on the Prize series, vol. 7, *The Time Has Come (1964–1966)*, 1990: Boston, MA: Blackside Inc. & Henry Hampton. Video on DVD.

37. Wisconsin State Historical Society, Miriam Feingold Collection.

38. Wisconsin State Historical Society, Miriam Feingold Collection 1965-6 Taped interview with AZ Young, Tape 1 Part 2. Transcription by author.
39. "Armed Defense," an Interview with Charles R. Sims, in Jay David and Elaine Crane (ed), *The Black Soldier: From the American Revolution to Vietnam* (New York: William & Morrow, Co., 1971), 195.
40. Ibid., 196.
41. Adam Fairclough, *Race and Democracy: The Civil Rights Struggle in Louisiana, 1915–1972* (Athens: University of Georgia Press, 1995), 342.
42. Lance Edward Hill, "The Deacons for Defense and Justice: Armed Self-Defense and the Civil Rights Movement," PhD Dissertation, Tulane University, 1997, 21.
43. Most of the leaders of the mainstream movement in CORE, the NAACP, and SCLC were touched by the military experience because of the draft, WWII, and Korea. Representative John Conyers of Michigan, Rep. Charles Rangel of New York, former Governor Dinkins of Virginia, and Harold Washington of Chicago are examples. Anecdotal evidence is that all the men in the DDJ had military experience as either draftees or war veterans. This was also the case with most of the Black Panther Party (BPP). Bobby Seale was an Air Force veteran, and most of the working-class men in the BPP were not allowed deferments. In Wallace Terry's Bloods, one of the oral histories is of a Vietnam vet who became a Panther, Reginald Edwards. He discusses his experience, and how he saw being killed in the Panthers by the police and being killed in Vietnam as the same on pages 11–12.
44. *US v Original Knights of Ku Klux Klan.*
45. Adam Fairclough, *Race and Democracy: The Civil Rights Struggle in Louisiana, 1915–1972* (Athens: University of Georgia Press, 1999), 362–63.
46. Ibid., 359.
47. FBI: Freedom of Information and Privacy Acts, Subject: Deacons for Defense and Justice, Part: 1 of 4, File number HQ 157–3290, Memorandum From J. H. Gale to Mr. Belmont Subject.: Deacons for Defense and Justice, dated March 15 1965, p. 49, accessed at http://foia.fbi.gov/ddj.htm as of April 12, 2005.
48. Henry Hampton and Steve Fayer, *Voices of Freedom: An Oral History of the Civil Rights Movement from the 1950s through the 1980s* (New York: Bantam Books, 1990), 287.
49. Roy Reed, "Armed Dixie Negro League is Spreading," *Des Moines Register*, Sunday, June 6, 1965, 8-G.
50. Ulysses Lee, *The Employment of Negro Troops. U.S. Army in World War II*, Special Studies (Washington, DC: Center of Military History, U.S. Army, 1990), 250–55.
51. Interview with Anderson, Dissertation, Selika Ducksworth, *What Hour of the Night: Black Enlisted Men's Experiences and the Desegregation of the Army During the Korean War, 1950–1*, Ohio State University, 1994, unpublished. Appendix.
52. Interview with Stewart, Dissertation, Selika Ducksworth, *What Hour of the Night: Black Enlisted Men's Experiences and the Desegregation of the Army During the Korean War, 1950–1*, Ohio State University, 1994, p. 267.
53. Interview with Predos, Dissertation, Selika Ducksworth, *What Hour of the Night: Black Enlisted Men's Experiences and the Desegregation of the Army During the Korean War, 1950–1*, Ohio State University, 1994, unpublished. Appendix.
54. Lance Edward Hill, *The Deacons for Defense and Justice: Armed Self-Defense and the Civil Rights Movement*. PhD Dissertation, Tulane University, 1997, 26.
55. "Armed Defense," an Interview with Charles R. Sims, in Jay David and Elaine Crane (ed), *The Black Soldier: From the American Revolution to Vietnam* (New York: William & Morrow, Co., 1971), 198.
56. See W. Fitzhugh Brundage's *Lynching in the New South: Georgia and Virginia, 1880–1930* (Urbana: University of Illinois Press, 1993), chapters 1 and 3 in toto. The literature on the Southern Code of honor and violence is extensive. Herbert Shapiro's *White Violence and Black Response from Reconstruction to Montgomery* (Amherst, MA: University of Massachusetts Press, 1988) is a wonderful source. David Chalmers' *Backfire* discusses the reactionary nature of the ad hoc violence, and how it was less deliberative in terms of thinking about reactions and implication in his introduction, and first chapter, as well as his conclusion.

57. "Armed Defense," an Interview with Charles R. Sims, in Jay David and Elaine Crane (ed.), *The Black Soldier: From the American Revolution to Vietnam* (New York: William & Morrow, Co., 1971), 191.

58. Ibid.

59. Fred Zimmerman, "More Dixie Negroes Buy Arms to Retaliate Against White Attacks," *The Wall Street Journal*, Vol. ClXVI, no. 7 (Monday, July 12, 1965), 1.

60. Ibid.

61. Hamilton Bims, "Deacons for Defense and Justice," *Ebony* (September 20, 1965): 28.

62. "The Deacons Go North," *Newsweek* (May 2, 1966): 20.

63. FBI: Freedom of Information and Privacy Acts, Subject: Deacons for Defense and Justice, Part: 1 of 4, File number HQ 157-3290, 8/4/65 Informant interview, p. 1, b7c, dated 8/17/65. Can be accessed at http://foia.fbi.gov/ddj.htm as of April 12, 2003.

64. Miriam Feingold, interviewer: CORE: Interview with Rowan Burris (tape in Miriam Feingold Collection) tape one track one, Wisconsin Historical Society, 1966.

65. George Lipsitz, "Introduction: Peace in the Struggle," in *A Life in The Struggle: Ivory Perry and the Culture of Opposition*, (Philadelphia:Temple University Press, 1988), 9–11. http://www.jstor.org/stable/j.ctt14bst0t.4.

Chapter Four

"The Military No More: Vietnam, Civil Rights, and Attitudes toward Change"

Jeremy P. Maxwell

In the initial stages of American involvement in Vietnam, black and white service personnel joined their respective services with the same sense of patriotism and duty that their predecessors had in prior wars. Having entered the armed forces during the period of integration, and in some cases before, African Americans believed it a better route to advancement and security than the civilian world could provide. Until the Vietnam War, that ideology was supported by the fact that civil rights leaders had made better progress on issues of equality and rights in the armed forces than they had in mainstream America. Integration, carried out in the military prior to the landmark Brown vs. Board of Education that provided for similar action in the civilian education system, was the most glaring representation of that ideal. By 1965, however, the United States assumed responsibility for the war in Vietnam and progress on equality within the military became stagnant. Significant changes to civil rights legislation and a more organized opposition to the status quo in the civilian world began to outpace similar advancements in the armed forces.

In June of 1970, journalist Wallace Terry wrote an article in the *Stars and Stripes* military newspaper entitled "The Growing Spirit of Militancy." In it, he claimed:

> Racial harmony between black and white American troops had disintegrated to the most dangerous level of the war.... Black soldiers are fed up with fighting and dying for what they consider a white man's folly... which stands in direct contrast to the black American fighting man of 1967 and 1968 who was anxious to prove himself in the most integrated war in U.S. history.[1]

He was publicizing the fact that the militant civil rights movements at home in the United States had a direct effect on the experience of soldiers and marines in Vietnam. According to him, "the combat volunteers of 1967 had been replaced by draftees and volunteers escaping a jail sentence stemming from their participation in racial conflicts at home, including ghetto upheavals."[2] While this may have been the case, it is important to examine what had changed politically in both civilian and military societies since the U.S. escalation in Vietnam. Owen Heggs, a black navy lieutenant serving during the Vietnam War, characterized the situation best when he asserted, "the immediate cause for racial problems in Vietnam was black people themselves. White people haven't changed. What has changed is the black population."[3] Institutional racism plagued African Americans throughout their experience in the military. Culturally biased battery tests, promotion and awards, and the military justice system were but a few of the problems blacks faced. The draft, however, was the initial hurdle young African Americans traversed that was marked by such prejudice. As the war continued, the ranks of the military were filled with draftees who had no desire to be part of the military complex they viewed as fraught with inherent institutional prejudice. Facing direct and institutional racism, this younger group of inductees questioned the motivations of the government, brought ideas inspired by the growing civil rights movement at home, and began to change the traditional African American view of the military as a path toward equality.

During Kennedy's short time as commander in chief, many African American soldiers were veterans of earlier wars and had come up through the military during the early stages of integration. Many were volunteers, as major escalation in Vietnam had not yet occurred. They expressed concern over the lack of promotions and the persistence of racist practices by commanding officers; however, they still viewed the military as the greatest opportunity for advancement over any other opportunities available in civilian society.

Donald Rander was drafted in 1961. Although the military was not his choice, he soon recognized that it was his best shot at a good life, as opposed to his situation at home, "where many of his friends were overdosing on drugs or getting killed on the streets of New York."[4] Similar attitudes toward the military were expressed even after American involvement in Vietnam was significantly increased. Chaplain Wesley Geary served in Vietnam from 1966 to 1967, and recalled that even then, "the military at that time or a government job . . . was the best thing that an African American could do in this country and probably for many, many years."[5] Antoine Roy enlisted in the army at roughly the same time. Citing a history of family members serving in the military since World War II and a belief that war builds men, matures you, and gives you the chance to prove yourself, Roy volunteered for a three-year enlistment with the provision that he be trained as a parachute infantryman and that he be sent to Vietnam.[6]

Despite the racism that still flourished among many high-ranking officers, and black participation being questioned by the African American civil rights leadership, many young black men still clearly viewed the military as an institution where they could rise up the ladder more than in civilian society. While that opinion clearly predominated, there was a schism coming for young blacks entering the service, polarizing race relations within the military.

Historians place the beginning of major U.S. involvement in the Vietnam War in 1965. President John F. Kennedy had been assassinated in November of 1963, which caused an outcry from the entire American population. African Americans viewed Kennedy as a progressive leader who would help promote equality. While Kennedy did have plans to work on civil rights, he never implemented major legislation to that effect. The most visible move for civil rights he made was signing Executive Order 10925 in March 1961 where the words "Affirmative Action" made their first appearance.[7] He also reconvened the President's Committee on Equal Employment Opportunity, the institution created during the Truman administration to facilitate the progress of integration within the armed forces. The committee became known as the Gesell Committee, named after its chairman, Gerhard A. Gesell, a well-known white Washington, D.C., attorney active in civil rights cases.[8] Although the committee lacked the authority it had received under Truman, Kennedy charged the group with examining two main questions:

1. What measures needed to be taken to improve the effectiveness of current policies and procedures in the armed forces with regard to equality of treatment and opportunity for persons in the armed forces?
2. What measures should be employed to improve equality of improvement for members of the armed forces and their dependents in the civilian community, particularly with respect to housing, education, transportation, recreational facilities, community events, programs, and activities?

A quick glance at the mandate given to the Gesell Committee makes it abundantly clear that Kennedy's moves on promoting equality during this period extended predominantly to the military. While the continuation of combating inequity in the armed forces was necessary—as moves toward equality in the military predated similar moves in civilian society—he did not make any similar impact on civil rights within society in America. Kennedy still coveted the African American vote but, like presidents before him, he hesitated to make any major moves on civil rights for fear of upsetting Southern Democrats who expressed vehement opposition to any such legislation. Fear subsided, however, when on May 2, 1963, the public safety commissioner of Birmingham, Alabama, T. Eugene "Bull" Connor, led policemen and firemen in an assault on African American marchers with attack dogs, nightsticks, and fire hoses. The brutal display—which was in fact, nationally televised—along with the murder of Medgar Evers (a NAACP state field secretary for the state of Mississippi who recruited members throughout Mississippi, organized voter-registration efforts, demonstrations, and economic boycotts of white-owned companies that practiced discrimination, and investigated crimes perpetrated against), prompted Kennedy to very publicly lobby for desegregation. Unfortunately, that mission, along with any future plans he might have had to enact civil rights legislation, was ended when he was assassinated.[9]

Greater moves on civil rights issues and a visible relationship with prominent African American leaders did come under Kennedy's successor, Vice President Lyndon Baines Johnson. Upon assuming the presidency, Johnson was faced with three very pressing concerns: the growing conflict in Vietnam, the need to solve domestic inequalities, and a campaign to hold the presidency in the election in the following year. Five days after Kennedy's assassination, "LBJ went before Congress and made it clear that he would pursue the slain President's legislative agenda."[10] By making such a promise, Johnson tied himself not only to matters of civil rights within the United States, but also to policies Kennedy was considering in Vietnam.[11]

Within the military, LBJ did not make a substantial impact on matters of equality. On June 24, 1962, Kennedy formed the President's Committee on Equal Opportunity in the armed forces to "investigate the status of minority groups, especially blacks, in the services and to see what progress had been made in the fourteen years since President Truman had decreed the end of segregation in the armed forces."[12] Kennedy charged the committee with examining two questions; what measures needed to be taken to improve the effectiveness of current policies and procedures in the armed forces with regard to equality of treatment and opportunity for persons in the armed forces, and what measures should be employed to improve equality of improvement for members of the armed forces and their dependents in the civilian community, particularly with respect to housing, education, transportation, recreational facilities, community events, programs, and activities?[13] In 1968, LBJ enacted the Fair Housing Act to prohibit discrimination concerning the sale, rental, and financing of housing based on race, religion, or national origin.[14] The Act, while important in finishing Kennedy's work concerning the military, was much more far-reaching in civilian society. In the immediate period following Kennedy's assassination, however, LBJ transmitted a letter with the final results of the committee to Secretary McNamara that effectively stated that "the Defense Department had done an excellent job in resolving many aspects of the general problem of discriminatory treatment of those who serve in the Nation's Armed Forces."[15]

LBJ was much more active concerning domestic affairs in civilian society. On July 2, 1964, he signed the Civil Rights Act of 1964, the most "sweeping legislation of its kind since Reconstruction." The Civil Rights Act prohibited discrimination on the basis of race, color, religion, sex, or national origin in public places, provided for the integration of schools and other public facilities, and made employment discrimination illegal. In a telephone conversation with prominent civil rights leader Martin Luther King Jr., Johnson called the Civil Rights Act, "the greatest achievement of his administration."[16]

LBJ declared a war on poverty and racism in the spirit of Franklin Delano Roosevelt (FDR), the president who had the greatest influence upon him and whom he admired the most. At the time, these two issues exemplified the issues facing African Americans and others who lived in poverty, and certainly provided a sound reason for blacks to support LBJ's candidacy for president. Unlike Roosevelt, however, and to some extent Kennedy, Johnson worked even closer with civil rights leaders to promote his position on such issues. LBJ worked closely with King, each using the actions of the other to promote their individual agendas. LBJ ran his campaign for the 1964 presidential election on a platform promoted as "The Great Society." In pressing the efficacy of his program, LBJ informed King that "8 billion of new health care, education, and poverty spending would benefit people that earn less than 2000 a year." LBJ's overarching goal was a set of domestic programs designed to eliminate poverty and racial injustice. While King remained reticent to fully trust Johnson, he judged him and past presidents almost completely, "by their concrete actions to advance the cause of civil rights."[17]

LBJ further expanded the scope of the Civil Rights Act a year later, by signing the Voting Rights Act of 1965 to overcome discriminatory practices that had prohibited African Americans from exercising their 15th Amendment right to vote. King had been pressing LBJ to make such moves since he took office. The two often colluded with one another, brainstorming ideas to ensure African Americans could avail of the Constitutional right. Collaboration between them served the interests of both men. Johnson recognized the necessity of strengthening the black vote to support his political agenda. King needed Johnson to continue to push civil rights legislation. In the year between the passing of the Civil Rights Act ant the Voting Rights Act, Johnson told King that he could contribute a great deal in highlighting the need for expanded legislation. His idea was that King should "find the worst condition that he could run into in Alabama and Mississippi or Louisiana or South Carolina . . . If you take that one illustration and get it on television, get it in the pulpits, get it in the meetings—every place you can—then pretty soon the fellow who didn't do anything but drive a tractor would say. 'Well, that is not right—that is not fair.' Then that will help us in what we are going to shove through in the end."[18] King agreed wholeheartedly that a great spectacle was needed to demonstrate prevailing inequities to the American public. One of most prominent examples of that common thinking was, when King led protesters in a march from Selma to Montgomery on March 7, 1965, in a peaceful protest designed to secure voting rights. Alabama state troopers responded by attacking them with nightsticks, tear gas, and whips after they refused to turn back. When the events of the day were broadcast on national television, King and LBJ had successfully demonstrated the inequities of the Jim Crow system to the American public.

Nor did LBJ stop promoting equality after signing the Voting Rights Act into law on August 6, 1965. A little over a month later, he issued Executive Order 11246 to establish requirements for non-discriminatory practices in hiring and employment on the part of the U.S. government. The order "prohibited federal contractors and federally assisted construction contractors and subcontractors, who do over $10,000 in Government business in one year from discriminating in employment decisions on the basis of race, color, religion, sex, or national origin." It also required contractors to "take affirmative action to ensure that applicants are employed, and that employees are treated during employment, without regard to their race, color, religion, sex, or national origin."[19] It superseded earlier orders that dated back to Executive Order 8802 that Johnson's hero, FDR, had enacted to prevent discrimination and promote equality in employment in the converted wartime production during World War II.

The collaboration between LBJ and King did not end with voting rights. The Civil Rights Act, the Voting Rights Act, and Executive Order 11246 were monumental achievements that signaled the potential for continued progress. To King and other civil rights leaders, however, that potential needed to be realized by continued action on the part of the government to ensure the domestic programs championed by Johnson were carried out. The growing situation in Vietnam, however, weighed heavy on the shoulders of Johnson and speculation over what issues would take precedence soon followed. It wasn't long before Vietnam was clearly the more pressing of the two, and that would prove to be the decisive issue that ultimately led to African American support for LBJ waning in the years that followed. It is important at this juncture to note that, while Johnson may have desired to pursue both the Vietnam War and the Great Society, he could have chosen one over the other at any point. He clearly made a decision.

The situation in Vietnam, presided over by Johnson, escalated aggressively. Under Kennedy, 16,300 American troops were present in Southeast Asia. When Johnson assumed the role of commander in chief, that number rose exponentially. By the time he authorized the sustained bombing campaign known as Operation Rolling Thunder, that number had expanded to more than 185,000, and it continued to climb until 1968, when it reached its apex at 536,000.[20] Increasing need for ground troops in Vietnam begged the question: How would the United States raise the necessary manpower to facilitate the expansion of the military, while maintaining a presence at bases it already had at home and overseas?

The military leadership had been arguing for the "need to mobilize reserve and National Guard troops to fill out the force structure," but LBJ remained hesitant on the issue of mobilization due to fears of possible objection on the grounds that there was no actual declaration of war.[21] He knew that by mobilizing such forces, many more Americans would know someone in uniform who might be impacted by the Vietnam War, which would likely translate into more intense antiwar sentiment. In the absence of a clear understanding of whether or not he possessed the authority to mobilize such units and fearing backlash for his refusal to request increased budgets, Johnson sought what he believed was the only remaining option available to him: to draft the forces he needed to prosecute his campaigns in Vietnam.

The draft would become a contentious issue for African American civil rights leaders. Initially, blacks were not being drafted in particularly high numbers with respect to their overall population. As those numbers grew, however, African American leaders attacked the draft for a number of reasons. The most glaring reason was its direct correlation to the number of black casualties in Vietnam. The likelihood that soldiers and marines would die in battle was not the issue with which prominent black leaders could not reconcile. Rather, they questioned why so many blacks had to die in Vietnam to protect the freedoms of the South Vietnamese when they did not enjoy the same freedoms at home. Why fight for the policies of the American government, when the American government would do little or nothing to promote equality at home?

Indeed, in the first years of the war, African Americans represented a higher proportion of casualties in Vietnam; however, African Americans were also more likely to volunteer for combat. According to SP4 Victor Hall, "blacks volunteered for combat due to monetary incentives like combat pay, and a faster route to promotion."[22] African Americans were also more likely to reenlist for the same reasons. According to information presented in the same newspaper article for which Hall was interviewed, the Department of Defense statistics show black reenlistment rates during the same period were three times that of whites.[23] As the draft drew in more young African Americans in the latter years of the war, however, those statistics significantly decreased, providing the reason for the roughly even overall proportion of black combat deaths. Nonetheless, the draft would continue to be a sore subject throughout the war, with claims of racial discrimination among other criticisms.

The draft would also represent the first point of contact with a military system that contained vestiges of inherent institutional racism. The Selective Service Act included provisions that allowed for a deferment system. The deferment system had been established to address the downsizing needs of the Defense Department in the wake of the Korean War. The services could no longer absorb the level of eligible inductees produced by the draft, so "college deferments became almost automatic, as did a variety of occupational deferments. Fathers were not inducted, and married men were placed in a lower priority category."[24]

The deferment program, while indeed a solution to the manpower issue in times of peace, was often subject to local prejudice and only served to illuminate social inequities in times of war. Subpar secondary education, coupled with a high percentage of families earning a low yearly income, prevented many blacks from being able to enter college to secure a deferment. Without an education and because of the prejudices that still permeated civilian society, single African Americans were also not likely to secure a deferment based on their occupation. To do so, they would have had to held jobs deemed vital to national security interests, such as physicists, engineers, or doctors, or jobs directly involved in war production. In 1972 Rev. Theodore M. Hesburgh, president of the University of Notre Dame and chairman of the United States Commission on Civil Rights, claimed that Americans of color had unequal access to better jobs because of reasons growing out of other inequalities, namely education.[25] Given that integration in schools was only carried out in 1954 and that African American schools prior to that received subpar funding, many African Americans were unable to secure those coveted jobs deemed of vital interest. These issues represented the unintended but inherent problems with the draft system manifesting at the local draft board, which showed direct racism was still present.

When an individual received a letter from the government informing them that they were being drafted, the process started with the draftee being ordered to present themselves to the local draft board. Local draft boards exercised a substantial amount of power, as it was their decision whether or not to issue a deferment based on occupation, hardship, or conscientious objection.[26] Some of the local draft board committees, particularly in Southern states, did not have any black members, and many had only a few. A 1964 Defense Department survey showed that among qualified men aged twenty-six to thirty-four, 30.2 percent of the blacks had been drafted in comparison with 18.8 percent of the whites.[27] Due to their inability to secure immediate deferments, young blacks came to represent a significant portion of the men challenging the local draft boards. When recalling his induction experience in Oakland, California, Stanley Goff stated that "at least 70 percent of the guys in his group were black, and that was a conservative estimate ... He felt strange waiting to be carted off to the military, and sat there thinking about slavery."[28]

Goff's feelings represented what many blacks felt: that the draft was being used as an effective means of thinning the black population by sending them off to war. The growing antiwar movement and African American opposition to the war capitalized on inequities such as this as the war progressed.

African American reactions to the draft were diverse. The militant and nationalist groups like those who followed the Nation of Islam (including Malcolm X) championed African Americans excluding themselves from a government that did not grant them equality, rather than working within the system to promote equality. The Student Nonviolent Coordinating Committee (SNCC) initially welcomed help from all who could help them protest for equality. That changed after 1965, when members decided that it would be best to prove that blacks could organize and sue for change on their own. A year later, SNCC leader Stokely Carmichael further highlighted the growing apathy toward passive resistance when he gave a speech after being released after his twenty-seventh arrest that elicited chants of "Black Power," a term coined earlier by fellow SNCC member Willie Ricks. The NAACP was equally opposed to the draft as the militant groups were, however, they spoke more toward the middle class within the African American population, whereas SNCC spoke to the poorer class; those more likely to fall subject to the draft and trouble with the legal system. All civil rights groups viewed the military as a racist institution. How could they not, given their historic fight to secure a place in the armed forces, and later struggle to combat segregation. More militant-leaning ideology during this period had a "profound influence on blacks who entered the service after 1965."[29] The formation of the Black Panther Party in 1966 served to further demonstrate that point, specifically the Ten Point-Program that guided their views on civil rights. Of the ten points, three were directly applicable to the military. Points six through nine called for all men to be exempt from military service, the end of police brutality and murder of black people, freedom for all black men held in federal, state, county and city prisons and jails, and that all black people brought to trial be tried in court by a jury of their peer group or people from their black communities, as defined by the Constitution of The United States.[30] While the former clearly indicated the apathy that some African Americans felt toward the military, the latter three were also related, since there was inequity in the military justice system and run-ins with the civilian authorities might lead to military service being part of sentencing.[31]

As the war continued to show no sign of abating, demonstrations against the draft included refusal to report to induction centers, the burning of draft cards, and a growing number of people claiming conscientious objection to the war. The most publicized case of draft resistance came on April 28, 1967, when world heavyweight boxing champion Muhammad Ali refused to step forward and be inducted into the army.

Born Cassius Clay, this sports celebrity changed his name to Muhammad Ali when he converted to Islam under the guidance of his mentor, Malcolm X. While he had originally been declared ineligible for military service, a change in army requirements in 1966 changed his status. Not wishing to acquiesce to the draft, he stated he had "no quarrel with the Vietcong. No Vietcong ever called me nigger."[32] He challenged the draft, claiming conscientious objection to the war in Vietnam based upon his status as a minister for Islam. Ali confronted the government and the Nation of Islam—whose leadership left him to fight his legal battles—in the very public and outspoken manner he had always maintained as a sports figure. His words, as the government feared, served as a wake-up call to young blacks of draft age, and a catalyst in the shift of African American antiwar rhetoric in the following years.

Martin Luther King Jr. had been the most outspoken leader in the African American community on the number of black deaths in the early years of the war. Initially, he refrained from publicly criticizing the war for fear of alienating LBJ, his most promising ally in the government on civil rights issues. That would change by 1967, as it became clear that more time and money was being spent on the war in Vietnam than on the Great Society programs that LBJ had promoted at home. Project 100,000 would make matters worse.

Project 100,000 was a Great Society program instituted in 1966 that was originally touted as a means of "providing training and discipline for America's disadvantaged youth."[33] In reality, the program lowered the military entrance requirements, making men eligible who would not normally have been accepted. Americans recognized the program as nothing more than a ploy to supply more troops for the war in Vietnam. They were also aware that the program directly affected the poor and disadvantaged, and not the well-to-do citizens who could secure medical or college-based deferments. What should have been readily apparent to LBJ and Secretary Robert S. McNamara (who oversaw the program) was that lowering the requirements on intellectual capabilities would have the reciprocal effect of presenting problems in training to those men once in the service. If they were not capable of learning technical job requirements, that only left one possible place for them to serve: the infantry. Though unknown to leaders like King in 1967, the overall statistics for Project 100,000 confirm that to be the case, since of the 350,000 men drafted under the program, 41 percent were African American, and 40 percent drew combat assignments.[34]

On April 4, 1967, Martin Luther King Jr. presented his "Beyond Vietnam" oratory before a crowd of three thousand at Riverside Church in New York City. Drawing the ire of LBJ as he had originally feared, King discussed a number of salient points that demonstrated the great deal of anguish he had felt over America's involvement in Vietnam up to that point, mostly in reference to the war on poverty he saw falling second to Vietnam. He concluded his oration with a series of steps he felt the government should take to extricate Americans from the war, including: ending all bombing in North and South Vietnam, declaring a unilateral cease-fire in the hope that such action would create the atmosphere for negotiation, taking immediate steps to prevent other battlegrounds in Southeast Asia by curtailing our military buildup in Thailand and our interference in Laos, accepting that the National Liberation Front has substantial support in South Vietnam and must thereby play a role in any meaningful negotiations and any future Vietnam government, and setting a date for the removal of U.S. troops from Vietnam in accordance with the 1954 Geneva Agreement.[35]

The public condemnation of the Vietnam War by both King and Ali irritated Johnson. However, African Americans had secured a modicum of progress in their fight against the draft when, by the beginning of 1968, black representation on draft boards had doubled. Whereas two years prior, blacks only accounted for 278 officials out of 4,080, they now numbered more than 600.[36] While that number did not signal a major change in terms of black representation, it was a step in the right direction. This advancement, coupled with the Vietnamization Policy instituted by the Nixon administration to hand back the war to the South Vietnamese, translated to the declining number of African American casualties in the war zone. While these were significant developments in relation to the draft and the overall casualty statistics, they did not slow the antiwar rhetoric that continued to flourish for the remainder of the war.

Opposition to the war and the military establishment itself steadily grew alongside developments on the battlefield. The government had been telling the American public that the war in Vietnam was nearing an end, until the Tet Offensive launched by North Vietnam on January 30, 1968, shattered that misrepresentation of the situation. Although African Americans had been making progress on the draft boards, and also in their struggle to secure places in the much-coveted safety of the National Guard, equality still eluded them within society and the military establishment.

The assassination of Martin Luther King Jr. on April 4, 1968, polarized the African American community even more, ushering in an era where antiwar protest reflected a more militant nationalist ideology than the passive resistance preached by King. MLK had been symbolic figure to both blacks and whites, as he was the face of the African American civil rights struggle. To African Americans, King was a hero, emblematic of the strength of character that blacks had to present throughout their struggle for equality. To some whites, however, King was a symbol of the movement attempting to unseat whites from their perceived position of privilege. It is no surprise, then, that King's death is generally recognized by historians as a crucial turning point when race relations in Vietnam took a significant turn for the worse.

The newer generation of draft-eligible blacks began breaking away from the traditional belief that African Americans who served in the military were proving their right to enjoy equality under the law. The new wave of inductees would enter the service with heavily politicized, revolutionary beliefs. This more militant ideology led to newspapers headlining their coverage with phrases such as, "Tensions of Black-Power Reach Troops in Vietnam," "Black Power Comes to Vietnam as Racial Tensions Increase," and indeed, Wallace Terry's "The Growing Spirit of Militancy."[37]

Protests of discrimination and, in several cases, riots between black and white personnel erupted throughout the military, not just in Vietnam. Confederate flags, Ku Klux Klan–style attire, cross burnings, and other "displays of hate and intolerance by white personnel fueled the growing hostilities between blacks and whites."[38] "At Cam Ranh Bay, whites hoisted a Confederate flag above the naval headquarters building after hearing the news of King's death."[39] To the many black draftees, such an act was a slap in the face. They were struggling for equality in the streets of America, drafted into a war they felt did not concern them. To them, the Confederate flag being flown at the base was a clear sign that their place in the military was not going to be any different than at home. Cam Ranh Bay was but one example of white troops parading in front of the Confederate flag. "As early as Christmas Day 1965, a number of white soldiers paraded in front of the audience at comedian Bob Hope's USO show at Bien Hoa Air Base and were later seen posing and taking photos under the flag."[40]

Visual representations of racism like this were particularly important since, as previously established, the beginning of full-scale American involvement in Vietnam commenced that same year. Those demonstrations served to further highlight that while integration had been completed in the military prior to the start of the Vietnam War, racism clearly prevailed. What changed was the response by younger, politically aware African Americans.

Riots were the most glaring representation of how far race relations had descended in Vietnam and further illuminated the apathy blacks felt toward the military. They were prevalent in country, at many overseas installations, and at home in the United States. The only areas during this period not plagued by large-scale riots were forward fighting combat units. A combat unit "had to gel as both a military unit and a homosocial group, individuals needed to believe that they could depend upon other infantrymen to hold their positions in a firefight."[41] "GIs and marines had to develop a greater spirit of unity in support of the common goal of survival."[42] Due to the constant threat of danger, or fear of death or dismemberment, issues of race receded to the periphery in the minds of these men.[43] In areas where the danger was not as acute, tensions between the races were more likely to reach a boiling point. Riots were typically found in rear areas, where black and white service personnel self-segregated themselves from one another. Frequent sites of unrest included Enlisted Men's clubs, other venues where alcohol exacerbated tensions, at brigs or stockades, and aboard ships where there was nowhere to escape.

On July 20, 1969, five marines were charged with murder after a race riot erupted at an Enlisted Men's (EM) club on the Camp Lejeune base in North Carolina when a black man tried to cut in on a white man dancing with a black woman.[44] A few weeks later, "two hundred men brawled in a free for all at Fort Bragg, North Carolina."[45] The official response was to deny that this clash was racially motivated. The frequency of similar outbreaks across the military, however, clearly undermined such claims. By the end of November 1969, Deputy Assistant Secretary of Defense for Civil Rights Howard Bennett was willing to admit that racial unrest was a "pervasive problem throughout the armed forces."[46] Despite acknowledgment by Pentagon officials like Assistant Secretary Bennett, serious incidents continued to spread across military installations at home and abroad.

Noteworthy episodes include a race riot at the Cam Ranh Bay Naval Station in Vietnam in 1969 and a fight between returning veterans at Kaneohe Marine Corps Air Station in Oahu, Hawaii. In 1972, a riot at Machinato, Okinawa, broke out "after MPs looked to arrest an African American GI suspected of involvement in a theft and assault."[47] Riots took place in U.S. bases in Germany and Canada. Military bases were not the only sites of discord.

Stockades were another place of frequent trouble. The military justice system had historically convicted and meted out disproportionately harsher sentences for African Americans accused of crimes over their white counterparts. Not surprisingly, riots sprang up in brigs and stockades at home and abroad, usually in relation to the antiwar movement, and particularly over issues of racial discrimination. Stockades were also unique in that inmates characteristically self-segregated themselves—as they did in the civilian penal system—based upon race.

In Vietnam, the two most noteworthy cases erupted at the marine brig in Da Nang, and at the Long Binh Stockade riot. Da Nang was the site of frequent rioting throughout the war. Yet a full-scale insurrection took place on August 18, 1968, after prisoners had become hostile as a result of a select number of inmates being transferred to alleviate pressures from overcrowding. The inmates had made claims of inhumane treatment to no avail, and they felt the removal of the chosen individuals was an attempt to silence their protests. During the riot, a group of MPs lobbed twenty tear-gas grenades at a group of unruly prisoners.[48] Before order was restored "prisoners held the compound for twenty hours, freeing seventeen inmates from the maximum security cellblock, and burning the facility."[49]

Prisoners revolted at a number of stockades during the same period. "The most publicized case of serious trouble in Vietnam was the Long Binh Stockade riot on August 29,1968, where militant blacks briefly took over a part of the jail."[50] Lasting two days, African American prisoners torched buildings and assaulted other inmates and guards to protest the unfair treatment by the stockade personnel who were predominantly white. At the end of the standoff, one prisoner had died, seven members of the custodial staff and twenty-six inmates required hospitalization, roughly the same amount received outpatient care, and four prisoners had escaped.[51]

Aside from clubs and stockades associated largely with ground troop personnel, African Americans in the navy faced similar issues. Naval vessels, much like stockades, were confined spaces that only served to exacerbate preexisting tension. Naval vessels and their associated ports of call were often the sights of significant racial discord. In a listing of racial events prepared for the Chief of Naval Operations spanning the period from August 1969 through the end of 1972, no less than twenty incidents, ranging from minor skirmishes to major riots, were reported as taking place.[52] John Sherwood, a historian at the Navy History and Heritage Command and author of *Black Sailor, White Navy: Racial Unrest in the Fleet during the Vietnam War Era* (2007), stated in an interview with *Navy Times* that the "Navy didn't suffer a lot of racial unrest in the 60's . . . Racial unrest in the Navy really started in 70's."[53] The majority of incidents occurred at base installations; however, two of the more publicized incidents at sea broke out aboard the USS *Kitty Hawk* on October 12, 1972, and the USS *Constellation* less than a month later on the first of November.

The official report on the events transpiring aboard the *Kitty Hawk* concluded that the causes of the riot were:

a. The sudden increase in the number of minority personnel entering the bottom of the hierarchical pyramid, with a very disproportionate fraction of minority personnel at the top of the pyramid, brought a perception of institutional racism.
b. The group psychology of a large number of minority personnel on each ship created new and different leadership challenges.
c. The directed elimination of discriminatory practices provided official confirmation that such practices had existed.[54]

Of the causes listed, the first point is particularly poignant when analyzed against the inequities of the draft system. There was a large number of minority personnel aboard the *Kitty Hawk* who held a lower enlisted rank. If a significant number of them were draftees who had come in under Project 100,000 after 1966, they might not have possessed the cognitive abilities previously thought necessary to perform the essential duties aboard the ship.

Equally problematic was that the *Kitty Hawk* had been serving in combat operations longer than the usual six-month rotation and drafted personnel did not want to be aboard in the first place. Those exigencies, coupled with racial tension permeating the military in the wake of the assassination of Martin Luther King Jr., led African American draftees serving aboard the *Kitty Hawk* in late 1972 to self-segregate themselves and section themselves off in different locations of the ship. According to Tom Dysant, a white sailor who enlisted in the navy to avoid the draft, "There was no noticeable racial tension. Life on board appeared to be just as segregated as in civilian life. There weren't any hard-and-fast rules about where blacks and whites could be, or any Navy-sanctioned separation of the races, but people just knew."[55] Self-segregation, prior instances of rioting, the perception of institutional racism, and the lack of command awareness of the overall situation aboard all combined to create the environment that led to disaster aboard the *Kitty Hawk*.

The events that transpired aboard the USS *Constellation* just under a month later were not nearly as hostile as those aboard the *Kitty Hawk*, however, they further illustrated the awareness of African American personnel to the inequities that characterized their situation. The *Constellation* had returned to San Diego after completing its sixth combat operations tour in Southeast Asia. While docked in July 1972 for extensive overhaul and repairs, the ship's crew went through a massive turnover of 1,300 personnel, 900 of which were new.[56] On October 4, 1972, the *Constellation* set out to sea for refresher training to test new equipment and train new personnel. Discrimination throughout the navy had been a growing topic of concern. While at sea, blacks "organized themselves to provide for an airing of their grievances, electing representatives and assigning specific functions to members of their group."[57] At the same time that black sailors organized to protest their concerns with perceived racism, the ship had to reduce its numbers by 250 to accommodate air wing personnel—those assigned to combat flight operations—that were needed aboard ship prior to the next combat deployment. Trouble ensued when a rumor spread that 250 sailors would be let go and would receive bad conduct discharges, and all of those would be black sailors.[58] While merely a rumor, it was clear to African American personnel that discrimination and racism would once again disadvantage them within the navy.

Outward demonstrations of a racist ideology and system that limited the opportunities for Africans Americans with respect to job placement, advancement, and equity within the military justice system only served to fan the flames of racial tension in Vietnam at and home. By 1968, especially, after the death of King, many African Americans viewed the military not as a path toward advancement, as their predecessors had, but as an institution wrought with inherent institutional racism. The draft was but a starting point; the first step into a larger system. It spelled the continuation of policies concerning Vietnam superseding civil rights issues at home and facilitated further injustices within the military that African Americans would have to endure. Other areas of military life were also affected by similar prejudice. Assignments and promotions, unequal practices in the justice system, and battery tests that did not account for differences in the socioeconomic backgrounds of enlistees and draftees also permeated the military complex. All of these prejudices served to turn African Americans away from the military as a path toward their greater cause of civil rights and look more toward avenues of protest in the civilian sector.

NOTES

1. Wallace Terry, "The Growing Spirit of Militancy," *Stars and Stripes*, June 30, 1970, 11.
2. Ibid.
3. "Black Power in Viet Nam," *Time*, September 19, 1969.
4. Yvonne Latty and Ron Tarver, *We Were There: Voices of African American Veterans, from World War II to the War in Iraq*. (New York: Amistad, 2004), 107.
5. Interview with Wesley Geary, 7 August 2009, Cantigny First Division Oral Histories II, Ohio University Libraries, http://www.library.ohiou.edu/cdm/images/cantigny/pdf/geary_wes_transcript.pdf.
6. Interview with Antoine Roy, undated, Antoine Roy Collection, The Vietnam Center and Archive, Texas Tech University, http://www.vietnam.ttu.edu/virtualarchive/items.php?item=OH0255.
7. Equal Employment Opportunity Commission, "Executive Order 10925," http://www.eeoc.gov/eeoc/history/35th/thelaw/eo-10925.html.
8. Jeremy P. Maxwell, *Brotherhood in Combat: How African Americans found Equality in Korea and Vietnam* (Norman: University of Oklahoma Press, 2018), 102.
9. Ibid., 103.
10. Ted Gittinger and Allen Fisher, "LBJ Champions the Civil Rights Act of 1964," *Prologue* Magazine 36, no. 2 (Summer 1964): 10.
11. Maxwell, *Brotherhood in Combat*, 107–8.
12. Henry I. Shaw Jr. and Ralph W. Donnelly, *Blacks in the Marine Corps* (Washington, DC: History and Museums Division, Headquarters, U.S. Marine Corps, 1975), 69.
13. Initial Report on the Equality of Treatment and Opportunity for Negro Military Personnel Stationed Within the United States, Box 106, The Edward M. Almond Papers, U.S. Army Military History Institute, Carlisle Barracks, Pennsylvania (hereafter referred to as the Gesell Report).
14. Ben Carson, "History of Fair Housing," U.S. Department of Housing and Urban Development, https://www.hud.gov/program_offices/fair_housing_equal_opp/aboutfheo/history.
15. Lyndon B. Johnson: "Letter to Secretary McNamara Transmitting Final Report of the President's Committee on Equal Opportunity in the Armed Forces," December 28, 1964. Online by Gerhard Peters and John T. Woolley, The American Presidency Project, http://www.presidency.ucsb.edu/ws/?pid=26772.
16. "Lyndon B. Johnson and Martin Luther King Jr. on 15 January 1965," Conversation WH6501-04-6736-6737, Presidential Recordings Digital Edition [Lyndon B. Johnson and Civil Rights, Volume 2, ed. Kent B. Germany] (Charlottesville: University of Virginia Press, 2014–). URL: http://prde.upress.virginia.edu/conversations/4005068.
17. Nick Kotz, *Judgement Days: Lyndon Baines Johnson, Martin Luther King Jr., and the Laws that Changed America* (New York: Mariner Books, 2005), 253.
18. "Lyndon B. Johnson and Martin Luther King Jr. on 15 January 1965," Conversation WH6501-04-6736-6737, Presidential Recordings Digital Edition [Lyndon B. Johnson and Civil

Rights, Volume 2, ed. Kent B. Germany] (Charlottesville: University of Virginia Press, 2014–). URL: http://prde.upress.virginia.edu/conversations/4005068.

19. "Executive Order 11246," National Archives, September 24, 1965, https://www.archives.gov/federal-register/codification/executive-order/11246.html.

20. Christian G. Appy, *Working-Class War: American Combat Soldiers and Vietnam* (Chapel Hill: University of North Carolina Press, 1993), 168.

21. John Prados, *Vietnam: The History of an Unwinnable War, 1945–1975* (Lawrence: University Press of Kansas, 2009), 151.

22. Gene Grove, "The Army and the Negro," *New York Times*, July 24, 1966.

23. Ibid.

24. James E. Westheider, *Fighting on Two Fronts: African Americans and the Vietnam War* (New York: New York University Press, 1997), 22.

25. Theodore M. Hesburgh, "Father Hesburgh's Program for Racial Justice," *New York Times*, October 29, 1972.

26. Paul T. Murray, "Blacks and the Draft: A History of Institutional Racism," *Journal of Black Studies* 2, no. 1 (September 1971): 69. For further information, see: U.S. Army Recruiting Command, "Qualitative Distribution Report of Male Enlistments, Inductions and Rejections," DD-MM663.

27. National Advisory Commission on Selective Service (1967) In Pursuit of Equity: Who Serves When Not All Serve? (Washington, DC: Government Printing Office, 1967), 22.

28. Stanley Goff, Robert Sanders, and Clark Smith, *Brothers: Black Soldiers in the Nam* (Novato, CA: Presidio Press, 1982), 1.

29. James E. Westheider, *The African American Experience in Vietnam: Brothers in Arms*, The African American History Series (Lanham, MD: Rowman and Littlefield, 2008), 25.

30. "What We Want Now!," *The Black Panther* 6, no. 6 (November 23, 1967): 3.

31. James F. Behr, "Vietnam Voices: An Oral History of Eleven Vietnam Veterans" (PhD Diss., Drew University, 2001), 27.

32. Max Wallace, "BACKTALK: Today's Athletes Owe Everything to Ali," *New York Times*, April 30, 2000.

33. Myra MacPherson, *Long Time Passing: Vietnam and the Haunted Generation* (Garden City, NY: Doubleday, 1984), 30.

34. David Coffey, "African Americans in the U.S. Military," in James H. Willbanks, *Vietnam War: The Essential Reference Guide* (Santa Barbara, CA: ABC-CLIO, 2013), 5.

35. Martin Luther King Jr., "Beyond Vietnam," speech given at the Riverside Church, New York, April 4, 1967.

36. Neil Sheehan, "Negroes Doubled on Draft Boards," *New York Times*, January 14, 1968.

37. The Associated Press, "Tensions of Black-Power Reach Troops in Vietnam," *New York Times*, April 13, 1969, 1–2; John T. Wheeler, "Black Power Comes to Vietnam as Racial Tensions Increase," *Washington Post*, April 20, 1969, 20; Wallace Terry, "The Growing Spirit of Militancy," *Stars and Stripes*, June 30, 1970, 11.

38. Westheider, *The African American Experience in Vietnam*, 75.

39. Westheider, *Fighting on Two Fronts*, 98.

40. Greg Grandin, "The Confederate Flag at War (But Not the Civil War)," *History News Network*, July 7, 2015, http://historynewsnetwork.org/article/159922.

41. Samuel W. Black, *Soul Soldiers: African Americans and the Vietnam Era* (Pittsburgh, PA: Senator John Heinz Pittsburgh Regional History Center in Association with the Smithsonian Institution, 2006), 5. See chapter 4, "Combat and the Interracial Male Relationship," in Herman Graham III, *The Brothers' Vietnam War: Black Power, Manhood, and the Military Experience* (Gainesville: University Press of Florida, 2003), 45–66.

42. Maxwell, *Brotherhood in Combat*, 121.

43. Maxwell, *Brotherhood in Combat*, 121.

44. "5 Marines Charged in Lejeune Killing," *New York Times*, August 8, 1969, 12.

45. "A Clash at Fort Bragg," *New York Times*, August 12, 1969, 23.

46. "Pervasive Racial Unrest Is Found in Armed Forces," *New York Times*, November 29, 1969, 1.

47. Westheider, *The African American Experience in Vietnam*, 101.

48. "Second Riot Quelled at Vietnam Brig," *New York Times*, August 19, 1969, 5.

49. "Marine Brig Hit by Riot at Da Nang," *Tuscaloosa News*, August 18, 1968, 28.

50. John T. Wheeler, "Black Power Comes to Vietnam as Racial Tensions Increase," *Washington Post*, April 20, 1969.

51. 720th Military Police Battalion Reunion Association Vietnam History Project, http://720mpreunion.org/history/time_line/1968/08_1968.html. *Time* reported on May 17, 1971, that 739 prisoners were present at the time of the riot, but the majority of sources cite 719 as the number. Long Binh was later updated to handle 600 prisoners, which would still have made it overcrowded on the day of the riot.

52. Listing of Racial Incidents with dates, locations, and other specifics, 1973, Folder 03, Box 01, Admiral Elmo R. Zumwalt, Jr. Collection: United States Navy, The Vietnam Center and Archive, Texas Tech University, http://www.vietnam.ttu.edu/virtualarchive/items.php?item=6320102049.

53. Mark D. Faram, "Race Riot at Sea—1972 Kitty Hawk Incident Fueled Fleet-wide Unrest," *Navy Times*, February 28, 2017.

54. "One officer investigation to inquire into the circumstances surrounding an incident of racial circumstances which occurred aboard USS *Kitty Hawk* on the night of October 12, 1972," 31 May 1974, Folder 01, Admiral Elmo R. Zumwalt, Jr. Collection: United States Navy, The Vietnam Center and Archive, Texas Tech University, http://www.vietnam.ttu.edu/virtualarchive/items.php?item=6320101025.pdf.

55. Gregory A. Freeman, *Troubled Water: Race, Mutiny, and Bravery on the USS Kitty Hawk* (New York: Palgrave Macmillan, 2009), 43.

56. Committee on Armed Forces, *Report by the Special Subcommittee on Disciplinary Problems in the U.S. Navy*, 92nd Cong., 2d sess., 1973, H.A.S.C. 92–81 (Washington, DC: Government Printing Office, 1973), http://www.history.navy.mil/research/library/online-reading-room/title-list-alphabetically/r/report-by-special-subcommittee-disciplinary-problems-us-navy.html#4.

57. Ibid.

58. Ibid.

Chapter Five

African American Leadership's Tug of War with Black Military Service Members

Rhetorical Situation Strategies in the Face of Gulf War

Elizabeth F. Desnoyers-Colas

Over two decades after the shocking defeat the U.S. military forces faced during the highly unpopular Vietnam War, the United States found itself leading a United Nations–authorized thirty-four-nation coalition force battling Iraqi forces who had invaded and annexed Kuwait on August 2, 1990. In January 1991, Operation Desert Storm, a 110-day military conflict, ultimately proved to be the most successful military victory since 1945, featuring three weeks of air attacks and 100 hours of ground war.[1] Prior to the launching of Operation Desert Shield/Desert Storm, however, President George H. W. Bush, the Congressional Black Caucus, African American civil rights leaders, black clergy, and other interest-focused antiwar/social activists and groups bitterly engaged in their own home-front battle in congressional and judicial halls and the national media. These U.S. civilian leadership factions clashed over what they deemed the real impact disproportionate numbers of and subsequent service of black troops who would deploy into Gulf War combat would have on the collective African American population. African American military service members accounted for 104,000 or 25 percent of the American troops in the Gulf during Operation Desert Shield and Storm while their demographic U.S. population numbers at home were 12 percent.[2] Seizing upon the disparity of these numbers, prominent African American leaders ominously predicted that twentieth-century U.S. war history would repeat itself; black troops would die in great numbers and would once again be "combat cannon fodder" (soldiers regarded or treated as expendable in battle)[3] as they were called during the Vietnam conflict when African American servicemen were 12 percent of the total deaths while 11 percent of the U.S. population.[4] These leaders claimed that post-Vietnam black service members of the vaunted All-Volunteer Force were actually an "involuntary modern day draft signee Armed Forces presence, a collective poverty level societal fraction of an "'economic conscription force.'"[5]

White House and Pentagon officials pushed back on the "cannon fodder" characterization claiming that the larger numbers of African Americans serving in the armed forces versus the numbers of whites, Hispanics, and other military members of color during the post–Vietnam War era were the result of a rise in patriotism and a random outcome of a "race neutral all volunteer force."[6] Joining in on that pushback was national journalists/media commentator Juan Williams, who accused these leaders of "casting the war in racial terms . . . driving a wedge between Black America and its troops in combat as well as main stream America which is strong in its support for Operation Desert Storm."[7] World War II and Vietnam African American veterans also fervently disputed the cannon fodder branding, defending black service members' collective eagerness and willingness to volunteer and expertly fulfill their duties as a large integral part of an integrated, well-trained professional military force.

Communication rhetorician Lloyd Bitzer defines rhetorical situation as discourse brought into existence by situation. It is a complex of natural contexts of persons, objects, and relations and an exigence which is an imperfection marked by urgency and which invites utterance.[8] The other two components of rhetorical situation are audience and constraint.

Military sociologist Charles Moskos explains the socio-political tug of rhetorical war of words and varied rhetorical strategies regarding African American over-representation in the Operation Desert Storm forces, stating

> Afro American attitudes toward the Armed Forces are extremely diverse and often contradictory. The black general public tends to have favorable views of the military, while the black leadership and intelligentsia tends to be more critical. . . . The black public regards the military as a secure place of employment and an honorable career in its own right. Military training is seen as a mechanism to instill discipline and often as a way to straighten out unruly youths. A negative view of military service is more typically articulated by black civil rights leaders and cultural figures.[9]

On the sidelines watching, reading, and listening to these arguments about their disproportionate military service responsibilities unfold these same troops were active-duty, U.S. Reserve, and National Guard, African American men and women service members of all ranks and services standing ready to prove themselves trained, fit, and Gulf War combat ready. Also standing with them were senior African American military leaders Joint Chiefs of Staff chairman General Colin Powell and Operation Desert Shield/Storm Deputy Commander in Chief for Operations, Lieutenant General Calvin Waller who were determined there would never be another Vietnam-type debilitating defeat of their country's armed force on their respective military watches.

This work closely examines a multitude of rhetorical situations waged by African American leaders (clergy, secular) and their black antiwar allies that underscored the potentiality of life-sacrificing vulnerabilities they perceived disproportionate numbers of Desert Shield/Desert Storm African American troops (lured by government promises of long-term career stability in a post-Vietnam All-Volunteer Force) would face during combat duty in the Gulf. In this essay, the exigence or the problems or issues examined and ultimately framed by the African American leaders' (clergy, civil rights, media) resulting rhetorical situations and strategies will primarily deal with their perceptions of Gulf War military service members and whether they should realistically be compared to the troops who were a part of cannon fodder lore during the Vietnam era. Their collective bleak argument as a rhetorical situation ultimately focused on one core belief: After eight years of African Americans seemingly finding themselves on the perceived negative receiving end of President Ronald Reagan's conservative economic agenda (known as Reaganomics and infamous for its cuts in government spending for crucial social programs, and services and the continuation of these policies by a similarly economically conservatively minded George H. W. Bush administration) these leaders reasoned that African American disproportionate voluntary military service could not be anything but economic exploitation, framed by inequality and racism, poverty, and a desolate work and labor force.

Meanwhile the African American service members' allies countered that rhetorical situation argument with views similar to those found succinctly delineated in a *Newsweek* Operation Desert Storm–related magazine feature piece, "The Battle for Respect," written shortly after the war.

> Desert Storm highlighted the military's stature as an instruction of opportunity for African Americans. Up and down the chain of Command, the war showcased a model of black achievement from Joint Chiefs Chairman Colin Powell to deputy Desert Storm Commander Gen Calvin Waller to three members of the Patriot missile crew decorated for shooting down Scuds over Riyadh. The rigid enforcement of antidiscrimination has placed unprecedented numbers of black men and women in positions of power winning them a legitimacy they find nearly impossible to duplicate outside of the service.[10]

This work revisits both sides of the arguments with a historical discussion of the All-Volunteer Force and its impact upon African Americans resulting in the growing numbers of black service members in the armed forces. African

American leaders (religious and secular) perceive harm of disproportionate military service of blacks in the Gulf and their rhetorical situation discourse keys in on fear of multiple black military deaths, dearth of domestic funding, and dissatisfaction of African American service members' role as global policing of oil countries The essay concludes with a refutation of the "cannon fodder" apologue by promoting a compelling argument to address the set of constraints that show how the conclusion of the Gulf War bought forth a new rhetorical strategy of defining the quality service tenor of African American military service in the course of their deployed mission

> The United States Military: Benefit in Peacetime, Burden during War.
> Since this country's beginning, military service order for its citizens has been to protect and uphold its values and loyalty to the nation by using militia troops and other configurations of temporary military forces to defend its interests. Public policy scholar David Armor claims debates over military representation are much older than the modern-day Civil Rights Movement, and they have risen in both draft and voluntary eras over the past two hundred years. . . . The oldest issue of military representation arises from the unique role and capability of an armed force, and the legitimate concerns of the populace about its motivations and allegiances. In a democracy, it is believed that a broadly representative military force is more likely to uphold national values and to be loyal to the government and country that raised it. For this reason, prior to World War II Americans were generally opposed to a large, permanent armed forces composed mainly of paid volunteer or "professional" soldiers.[11]

Since the Revolutionary War, African Americans have especially also served with "unwavering unassailable patriotism"[12] to prove their loyalty and willingness to uphold its country's values in order to attain long-awaited equal rights. However just as in previous generations of African American military service in American wars, black servicemen of the civil rights era (especially those who were drafted) still did not feel that they had attained equality but would remain second-class citizens despite their showing of patriotism. Coupled with that realization was African Americans' prevailing view that the U.S.'s overreliance on the military draft to eradicate communism and fight for freedom for the Vietnamese while overlooking inequality for blacks in the United States on the home front became the ultimate civil rights irony.

In January 1969, former President Richard M. Nixon developed what eventually became today's All-Volunteer Force. Nixon wrote a memorandum to Secretary of Defense Melvin Laird stating ". . . It is my firm conviction that we must establish an all-volunteer armed force after the expenditures for Vietnam are substantially reduced."[13] Initially few believed that African Americans would take advantage of this new military service program. Military analyst Martin Milkins notes that since the genesis of the All-

Volunteer Force (AVF) in 1973, African Americans have joined the armed forces more than three times that of whites.[14] Those who became a part of the post-Vietnam (and later during the Operation Desert Shield Desert Storm era of the 1990s) military were African Americans from the middle-class sector and were more higher educated than their white counterparts. Many of them had joined the military to receive a college education, travel, receive better pay advances, and take advantage of a wider range of employment opportunities and career mobility as officers or enlisted. African American women were able to serve in a wider capacity and receive more opportunities for promotion. All of the Volunteer Force members were higher qualified, easier to train, and had better morale dispositions than their drafted Vietnam-era African American counterparts. Author Gail Buckley elaborates, noting

> When the All-Volunteer Force was born, the unofficial Army slogan was "no more Vietnams. Nor more drafted, with their economic loopholes, leaving in the main bottommost strata of service to serve. Uncle Sam now wanted motivation, not just bodies. The military wanted young people who were looking for job training, travel opportunities and college funds. . . . in the years immediately after the Vietnam War when most middle class white American youth had come to profoundly distrust the military, it was predicted of the volunteer service would attract dispportionately high numbers of minorities. ROTC recruitment had stepped up at black colleges after white campus units closed in the wake of Vietnam protests. In 1973, blacks formed about 17 percent of the enlisted military as a whole. By the late 1970s, the proportion had nearly doubled.[15]

A big part of the recruitment and retention draw to AVF and especially to Desert Storm troops proved to be the military's long-standing model of meritocracy and equality. *Meritocracy*, a term first used in 1958, typifies how a military has made a transition to allowing people to advance through ranks and assignments based on their abilities, rather than their skin color or gender or any conventional business model quota system. Secretary Laird's additional taskings to ferment the attributes of the AVF was to help to effectively create and sustain a military force that would implement fair race practices and equal opportunity in order to help the overall mission advance in war and peacetime. In 1972, Laird addressed the Congress on the impact of the undertaking of that task.

> Let me candidly tell you that we face formidable problems in the manpower area that are not going to be solved overnight. In addition to complex recruiting and retention problems we share with the rest of American society, the agonizing problems related to race relations . . . We in the Department of Defense are determined to continue leading the way, as best we can, in making solutions to these difficult problems.[16]

When it appeared that the AVF would suffer potential program-killing political troubles, African American leaders strenuously argued in favor of black troops actually taking part in these new forces primarily to staunch the fears of recalcitrant white politicians scared that this new military would become "too black." For example, former New York Congresswoman Shirley Chisolm suggested that the concerns about the United States fostering a too black army were merely "deep fears of the possibility of one." At the same time, African American Congressman Ronald Dellums was also an early fan of the AVF; he didn't see a problem with it. Dellums specifically noted that black servicemen who wanted to join the military would do so on their own as individuals, not because they were forced to do so by their country. Just as the United States offers men and women the freedom to be whom they choose, they could freely join the military knowing the risk they would take to do so. Despite the support of these two African American congressional leaders, there were liberal and conservative white and black detractors. Conservative Senior Fellow Cato Institute Doug Bandow asserts that these early detractors of AVF would be proven wrong about how this program's military service worth to the country and to the African American community would eventually fare, especially when it successfully peaked in the mid 1980s:

> The military had had no trouble filling its ranks with top-quality people— young men and women who are in fact better educated and brighter than their civilian counterparts. During the first year of fiscal year 1990 for instance, 91 percent of new recruits had graduated from high school, compared with 75 percent of all 18 to 24-year olds; 96 percent of enlistees scored in the top three (of five) categories of the Armed Forces Qualification Test (AFQT), compared with just 69 percent of civilian youth. The military achieved comparable results through the 1980s, despite predictions that continued economic growth would make recruiting difficult.[17]

In 1990, the AVF was firmly entrenched as the African American components of the armed forces drew from these percentages of quality service members to boost its numbers. The rapid growth of African American numbers in the All-Volunteer Force however eventually became the proverbial thorn in the side of selected black clergy and civil rights leaders.

PREACHING TO ANTI–GULF WAR CHOIR: AFRICAN AMERICAN CLERGY PROTEST DESERT SHIELD/STORM

Historically, the collective African American church has served as the spiritual and societal bastion of the communities and people it serves. Therefore, it is no coincidence that the collective black church took such great interest in the number of African Americans who would ultimately serve and deploy during any given military conflict. Several prominent black bishops and pastors were some of America's first clergy to create their rhetorical situation strategies and speak out against the war, specifically against the disproportional number of African American service members' deployment to the Persian Gulf. In 1990–1991 the seven major mainstream Protestant African American denominations had a 900,000-membership roll (this large black national audience was a potentially significant constituent part of their rhetorical situation and strategy) and their pastors could conceivably reach 1.9 congregants weekly with their messages.[18] According to commentator Arch Puddington (former aide of civil rights leader Rustin Bayard), these leaders and their congregations were actually more likely to hold those who were in the military up as shining examples of thousands of young employable African Americans who were successful in their military service and in the positive throes of upward mobility because of it.[19] Part of that pride emanating from the pulpit and shared with the congregants in the pews focused on what black *Chicago Tribune* columnist Clarence Page describes as African Americans' steadfast military service. African American service members typically showed high enlistment and lower attrition rates than whites. African American women showed the lowest attrition rates of white men, white women, and black men.[20] In that light because of the shared pride in these accomplishments, the majority of African Americans' clergy initially did not publicly complain or protest about the number of black troops serving in any of the armed forces branches until the advent of the Desert Shield buildup of troops in August 1990. As more and more of African American service members began to deploy to the Gulf, however, black clergy leadership became increasingly concerned and started revisiting the old worrisome rhetorical situation paradox from the 1960s: Once again African American troops were being deployed to free one country (this time Kuwait) from another (Iraq) while African Americans still suffered inequality at home. In that light, African American clergy quickly took moral and spiritual leadership stances against the war particularly during its early buildups as they watched many of their congregants (even fellow clergy) deploy in large numbers. Clergies' collective' rhetorical strategy and framework of protest focused on several issues. First, they concentrated on the inequitableness the disproportionate numbers of deployed African American troops would bear and the plethora of dangers they faced during the Gulf War. They also framed their continued grievances towards addressing the severe domestic problems negatively affecting African American communities nationwide, problems that were not being sufficiently addressed by White House funding budgets and were now being more ignored because of the impending war. One part of their argument was that there would not be sufficient funds military personnel returning from the Gulf would need for health care needs, housing, and education. Why should African Americans serve if these needs in their communities were not going to be met? As the Operation Desert Shield Storm buildup continued, in October 1990 George H. W. Bush dealt the African American community what was perceived as another severe setback when he vetoed the 1990 Civil Right Bill, a major antidiscrimination bill.[21] The bill would have expanded job protections that had been removed by six U.S. Supreme Court cases and scale back a ruling the Court had made, causing it to be more difficult to win cases charging that job requirements or employment practices resulted in discrimination even if unintended. George H. W. Bush became the second president in the twentieth century to veto a civil rights piece of legislation (President Ronald Reagan was the first). African American clergy supporting the civil right bill bitterly claimed his veto was a victory for businesses and corporations, but a resounding defeat for black troops sacrificing for the country. Baptist pastor Reverend Samuel McKinney (a Morehouse College classmate of Reverend Martin Luther King Jr. and a pastor of Seattle's Mount Zion Baptist Church in Seattle) best expressed this collective protest view by wryly noting, "Thirty percent of the troops in Saudi Arabia are African Americans. I don't know why the president went over there to have Thanksgiving with them when he could have stayed here and signed the Civil Rights Bill."[22]

When Reverend T. J. Jemison, then president of the National Baptist Convention and leader of the 7.8-million-member denomination spoke out at the convention against the Gulf War, he plainly cited an immoral "war over oil" controversy and the drain the war has on domestic funds in poor communities as his chief reason for wanting African American service members not to have to serve disproportionally in the Gulf War.

> There is a moral issue . . . it's over oil. We are jeopardizing our fine men and women over oil in the Persian Gulf. We're not fighting over any principle or ideal . . . It's unfortunate America would become involved . . . Think of the good that a billion dollars could do for black Americans . . . and poor white Americans.[23]

National Baptist Reverend Charles G. Adams (Detroit mega church pastor of 7,000-member Hartford Memorial Baptist Church) was another initial African American Church denomination leader who spoke out against military intervention in the Gulf, noting that the U.S.'s focus should be on domestic issues such as curbing drug cartel activity in the United States than "to go to war on behalf of oil cartels."[24] In February 1991, during a National Emergency African American Leadership Summit held in Harlem's historic Abyssinian Baptist Church, John Hearst Adams, senior presiding bishop of the African American Episcopal Church, spoke of "being deeply disturbed by the racial immorality" of the Bush administration waging war in the

Middle East while not doing anything further about the problematic domestic U.S. issues.[25]

In African American Catholic circles, clergy also made their concerns known about black troops serving disproportionately in the Gulf War. Reverend Father George H. Clements of Chicago's Holy Angels Catholic Church called for an immediate stop of the war after announcing that he regretted urging young people from his parish to enter the military. There were times he would even look in local telephone books for the numbers of military recruiters and give the young parishioners cab fare to get to them because some of his young parishioners were poor and could not find jobs. To Father Clements it seemed at the time like the only avenue was joining the military. But not if it meant dying in a war while the country ignored domestic issues at home, he reasoned.

> The majority of these youngsters that are out there did not volunteer to go out to somebody's desert to fight . . . they volunteered to struggle against the lack of education. They say we should be proud to fight for our country. Yes, if my country were actually a nation that was fair to everybody then I would have been proud but that is not the case.[26]

As a black church attender, the nation's first black president, Barack Obama, says he has grown to recognize the importance and the necessity of the collective African American Church and the multitude of roles it plays in black communities to meet pressing social needs. Part of that understanding of its importance has come from culling situational messages gleaned from the rhetoric preached by African American pastors like his former pastor Jeremiah Wright to frame his own rhetorical commander in chief focus on how troops are used in war and peacetime. Like Obama, military members and their families have that spiritual legacy to draw and depend on regardless of their own personal views about perceived overrepresentation of military service.

THE KING FAMILY: OVERCOMING WAR WITH THE NONVIOLENT LEGACY

Protesting against war and advancing the prospect of peace has always been a stalwart part of the rhetoric of several civil rights icons who worked with and closely followed Martin Luther King Jr's nonviolence philosophy. Predictably, several civil rights leader icons who spoke out and developed their own rhetorical situations and used it to speak out forcefully against the Gulf War. Coretta Scott King has been an antiwar activist and strong proponent for peace since her undergraduate college days at Antioch College in Ohio. For example, she was a part of the creation of the National Committee for a

Sane Nuclear Policy in 1957 and represented Women's Strike for Peace at a nuclear-disarmament conference in Geneva in 1962. She stepped out into the foray of speaking out against U.S. involvement in the Vietnam War before her husband began to publicly oppose the war in 1967. In 1965, she addressed an antiwar rally at Madison Square Garden, in New York.[27] Three weeks after her husband's assassination she led an antiwar rally in New York's Central Park. Shortly after the Kuwait invasion, Coretta Scott King, now as leader of the King Center in Atlanta and gatekeeper of her husband's nonviolent antimilitarism philosophy, began her antiwar activism against the Gulf War. First, King immediately began her protest against the war by writing and publishing though national media a series of position papers and giving countless interviews to major media and other antiwar publications and media outlets. Her main assertion against the war was that the United States nor any nation should not engage in it. She urged the United States to follow the edicts of the sanction written by the United Nations August 6, 1990. The King Center released the following resolution to formally bring about this request:

> NOW Therefore be it resolved that the King Center further calls on the United States Government to refrain from making any further military commitments to address this crisis and to instead apply all U.S. political and economic leverage to support United Nations sanction. The King Center further call for immediate demobilization of military forces in the Gulf, accompanied by UNITED Nations–mediated negotiations between disputant nations. The King Center pledges its wholehearted support for creative nonviolent, conflict resolution of this crisis that can benefit all of the people of the Middle East and lay the foundation for a new era of regional friendship, cooperation and a more peaceful world.[28]

To solidify a key part of the King Center protest, Coretta Scott King took pages from her husband's civil rights rhetorical playbooks of the 1960s by calling for civil disobedience that would fill up the jails, endless marches and other civil-disobedience-type challenges that could be launched against all national government policies that promoted the use of the lives of thousands of Americans in "blood over oil" military engagements in the Middle East. Instead of using the more than $140 billion reliable sources she knew predicted the war would end up costing, the monies should be used for domestic issues at home (e.g., education and job training). "We cannot eradicate illiteracy and other social problems. . . . until we eradicate the scourge of militarism from the face of the earth."[29] Also, she urged Americans to write Congress and the president to urge them to declare a cease-fire. She also called for a nationwide antiwar movement launch that would ideally last until peace in that region of the world was assured, declaring that in the name of her husband who dreamed of peace, "there would be no more fitting tribute to his memory . . ."[30] She also used her husband's antiwar rhetorical strategy to press Georgia State black legislators and U.S. Representatives to join in her cause and spread her nonviolent message.

Martin Luther King III, an Atlanta-area Fulton County Georgia Commissioner, also spoke out against the war on behalf of the King Center. His rhetorical situations aimed at African American military members and other black leaders were more incendiary and mutinous than those coming from the King Center or his mother, yet they too espoused nonviolence. His speech, given to an audience at Operation PUSH in Chicago in 1991, again reiterated the long-held perception that African Americans have historically fought around the world to attain everyone else's freedom, yet the equality blacks yearned for themselves as Americans has not yet been realized. It was time for them to stand up for themselves and demand their government spend the necessary funds to meet their domestic needs that were not currently being met. He urged

> We've been fighting a war we've been told to fight and right here in the United States we don't have rights . . . Every black soldier ought to say "you all do what you want to. I'm not gong to fight." This is not my war. . . . I don't know what you achieve dropping bombs on another country . . . violence begets violence. We Americans or more specifically members of Congress almost did not pass the budget this year yet we were able to go over to Iraq, no matter how much it costs.[31]

The King family protested the war through various programs and events held at the King Center and by joining marches in Atlanta and nationally. Using the same rhetorical platform, Mrs. King continued urging the president and other world leaders to bring the war to an end. Despite their continual dedicated rhetorical use of the nonviolence ideology developed by her husband and other civil rights leaders/clergy of like minds, King family did not specifically take a position against African American troops serving but instead showed concerned about their domestic conditions and those of their families. When asked, Mrs. King generally urged people to support the troops but not the war, which was a common mantra of support used by antiwar activists of Operation Desert Storm that Juan Williams likened to "words mouthed to put a smiley face on opposition to the war."[32]

SETTING THE CAPTIVES FREE: JESSE JACKSON HOSTAGE NEGOTIATOR, ANTIWAR PROTESTOR

Another civil rights leader who was against the war and engaged in nonviolent protest to bring the African American troops home was Jesse L. Jackson Sr. Like Coretta Scott King and King Center staff, he immediately began his protests against the U.S. policies regarding the war early August 1990. Jesse Jackson (and other African American leaders) were upset with President Bush because he had not met with African American leaders like other U.S. presidents (e.g., Franklin Roosevelt, Harry S. Truman) to discuss how the war policy for the Gulf intervention would be made. In Jesse Jackson's case, as Washington D.C. Shadow Senator in the U.S. Senate 1991–1997 (he had run for U.S. president as a Democratic candidate in 1984 and 1988) and popular African American leader, he felt he spoke for not only black Americans but for all Americans. Against the advice of the State Department, and President Bush, Jackson went to Iraq (after they lifted a travel advisory hold against travel to that region) to try to use his humanitarian influence to free 237 international hostages (forty of them Americans) being held as human shields. During that trip, Jackson met with Hussein and conducted a television interview that would air upon his return to the United States. Hussein's interview was viewed as a propagandist message that heavily favored Hussein's personal stance of his invasion of Kuwait but the end result was that 237 hostages were released to Jackson and bought back to the United States. Like the Kings in 1990 and 1991 Jackson used his rhetorical situation being frequently quoted in the national media castigating President Bush's war policies. He also spoke at protest rallies, one with Former N.O.W President Molly Yard, peace activist and Department of Defense whistleblower Daniel Ellsberg, and Republican U.S. Senator Charles Grassley.

Jackson's situational rhetoric antiwar rhetoric primarily centered on the futility and dangers of military conflict especially for the disproportionate amount of African American troops that were serving in the Gulf. As the D.C. shadow Senator, his biggest concern was that the district had more military members in the Gulf than forty-seven states; many of them were African American. Jackson's battle against the war also dealt with the question of why the United States should continue to play global police force when there were no military conflicts in Northern America. "There were no troops in Canada on our border about to bomb us," he noted, in an appearance on Black Entertainment Television shortly after the war began. While not as extreme as Martin Luther King III's call for mutiny, Jackson darkly complained about the president's veto of the civil rights bill, claiming it as a primary reason African American troops should not trust their civilian leadership to take care of them and their families at home. He testily stated " . . . They've got a commander in chief who vetoed the civil rights bill. It raises great questions back here at home about how we can keep morale up . . . Bush is color conscious when it comes to keeping blacks out of jobs but colorblind when it comes to sending us to the front line."[33] Days before the war started in 1991, Jackson shouted to an overwhelmingly black audience: "If that war breaks out, our youth will burn first." Like African American clergy and other civil rights leaders, he outlined the economic sacrifice people of color traditionally face that could have driven them to sign up for military service, noting, "In peacetime, blacks and Hispanics find opportunities in the military not available to them in civilian society. With the advent of the war, those benefits to heavy burdens as sacrifices fall so unevenly."[34] Ironically Jackson felt his work with antiwar protestors and his international call for the end of the war did not stop him from showing his support for the troops. Like Mrs. King, he suggested he genuinely supported the troops and even understood the why behind African American service members feeling they had to sacrifice. "How can it be that those of us who want to bring them home safe and walking in their shoes and not in body bags support them any less than those who do?" Some African American service members no doubt found his support claim dubious, later suggesting he and other black leaders who espoused the antiwar viewpoint and embraced the cannon fodder ideology did not support them.

Joseph Lowery: History Will Vindicate Us

Another prominent civil rights leader and associate of Martin Luther King Jr., Joseph Lowery also used similar Dr. King nonviolent rhetoric along with his position as the leader of the Southern Christian Leadership Conference to speak at rallies and churches against the war. He joined other black leaders and frequently spoke against the disproportion of African American troops in the Gulf War. Lowery had been a longtime proponent and practitioner of the nonviolence philosophy and felt the Bush administration had made a grave error in engaging in war and not allowing the U.N. sanctions to do the work in convincing Iraq to leave Kuwait. When President Bush announced in November 1990 that he was going to give Iraq until January 15, 1991, as a withdrawal date, many black leaders took great affront to the administration using King's birthday as a date to launch war. On January 15, 1991, Lowery, speaking to 2,000 people in Atlanta, bristled with outrage about the "Insensitivity of the George Bush administration . . . which did not recognize the inappropriateness of utilizing January 15th, the birthday of the advocate of peace, as the deadline in the sand. . . ."[35]

In February 1991, Lowery met with forty-nine other African American clergy and civil rights leaders to form a coalition that continued protesting the war, in particular chiding President George Bush's refusal to take Sadaam Hussein's offer to withdraw from Kuwait. "I'm disappointed in our government's response to what we believe is a timely opportunity to put an end, or at least call a moratorium to the war. There is nothing more to prove by a continuing military assault on Iraq and Kuwait."[36] The coalition had been chastised by supporters and even dissenters of the Bush administration for not standing by the country when it was at war. They too were accused of possibly driving a wedge between African Americans and whites. Undaunted, Lowery remembered the price Martin Luther King Jr paid and the ridicule he suffered nationally when he spoke up against the Vietnam War. Lowery mentioned that he was one of the few who stood by King during those difficult times. Those who followed King at that time were accused of bringing the same type of societal division. Lowery said when it came to this particular war in the Gulf he would stand confident and firm: ". . . history vindicated the dissenters in Vietnam, and I think it will vindicate us." As a part of this coalition's plan of action they urged churches to serve as sanctuaries to war resisters and to help military members take the steps to become conscientious objectors. As a master of rhetorical symbolism, he went to Philadelphia to attend a peace ceremony, tolled the Liberty Bell eight times and offered this benediction: "Let us call upon the nations to spend our resources on medical supplies, buy bread to feed the hungry and build houses, not foxholes." Even in his call for peace, and his publicly expressed frustration with President Bush for not waiting longer on the sanctions to take effect, Lowery recognized that Saadam Hussein needed to know that his country's invasion of Kuwait was wrong and he had to be dealt with. The Congressional Black Caucus however did not share his peace-generating sentiments.

Congressional Black Caucus: No Black Blood for Oil

In 1990, there were twenty-six Democrats and one Republican in the Congressional Black Caucus (CBC). In CBC home districts many of their constituents also were concerned about the disproportionate amount of African American troops who deployed to the Gulf War and frequently shared their concern with the CBC. From the beginning of the war buildup, the CBC had already joined other African American leaders letting the president know their displeasure about his vetoing the 1990 Civil Rights Bill, a veto they felt would ultimately harm the overall African American communities, especially those in them who were jobless, homeless, and not able to get the education they needed. U.S. Representative Charles Hayes (D-Ill) helped shape the rhetorical structure many of his colleagues and other black leaders shared about disproportionate African American troop service in the Gulf War: "I don't see any fairness at all in a president vetoing a civil rights bill that would have given African Americans an equal opportunity for employment, and having a disproportionate number defending a system where they can't even find a job . . . to me that it's not right."[37] Representative Maxine Waters (CA, D), a member of the House's Veterans Affairs Committee and a very outspoken critic of the Bush administration, more forcefully spoke out against the war, leveling her anger at the president about the all too real possibilities of high black troop Gulf War causalities because of racist Republican White

House policies. Waters claimed that many of the African American constituents and servicemen and women from all over the country she met told her:

> It is not fair for me to maybe have to volunteer the military to be educated, to get trained, to have a job . . . Something's wrong in America that does not provide me with an opportunity for a better quality of life job, to have a roof over my head. Something's wrong in an America that does not provide me an opportunity for a better quality of life. And there is certainly something wrong when it appears that the people in charge of the debate, particularly the president of the United States, use their power to foster racism and discrimination rather than eliminate it.[38]

As far as Waters was concerned, the Gulf War was just another example of the Bush administration willfully fostering social and economic inequality for African Americans, therefore they should not have to serve in a war for another country's freedom if they did not get equality at home. "It is not anybody's war to fight, but most definitely it's not African American's war to fight . . ."[39] Along with Waters, other CBC members immediately shared their concern not only about these possible high casualty numbers but the continued advancing of AVF policies that had helped to produce these figures in the post-Vietnam era. International law scholar Henry Richardson III noted that CBC members like Jackson were angry that they were left out of the political-making loop especially when it came to establishing policy that best outlined the overall interests of African American troops and how they would be strategically used as part of mobile militia-type forces undertaking a foisted upon responsibility "policeman of the world "role on behalf of the United States. This political snub from the Republican administration did not set well with the CBC, especially with then CBC Chair Ronald Dellums (D-CA). Richardson observes

> Save for a few individuals (beyond General Colin Powell) we in Afro America were not included in the policy debates and decisions either before or during the gulf crisis. We only participated peripherally in resolving the constitution question of authorization to dispatch U.S. Troops against Iraq when the Congressional Black Caucus voted unanimously (with one exception) against the resolution of January 12, 1991 . . .[40]

As congressional debates grew more heated prior to the vote regarding authorizing the use of force against the Iraqis, CBC speeches against the war given on the House floor became more strident and heated. New York Representative Major Owens who had the second largest district holding African American service members spoke of "slaughter in the desert." In his speech he outlined his opposition to the war:

> "My conscience tells me that if I vote for all of the unnecessary killing, this mass murder, I become an accessory to murder and said his vote against the war would help save those in his district who were deployed. "I don't want to see the bravery, the loyalty and dedication of these soldiers trashed."[41]

Eleanor Holmes Norton, a Washington D.C., delegate to Congress, was harshly criticized by Washington D.C., print and newspaper journalists for criticizing the war and as a result took to the House floor several times to speak about the disproportionate amount of African American troops that she represented from the D.C. area that did not have a recognized voting voice in Congress to speak for them. Once on the floor she noted:

> .... Like voting representation in Congress, race should not be and never has been off limits during wars. . . . None of us should feel comfortable with a peacetime volunteer army with large racial disproportions that can be converted to a wartime army in which those who die also could be greatly disproportionate.[42]

Black Caucus members were also very skeptical about the true purpose of the war, echoing the rhetorical context of other African American leaders by steadfastly maintaining that the U.S. involvement in Gulf War[43] was really about managing and stabilizing the region's oil wealth. Rep. Charles Rangel (D-NY) sardonically termed the U.N. coalition's attempts to free socially oppressive Kuwait from being annexed by Iraq as "dipstick diplomacy that says we must expose our young people to death for oil," while Congressman Gus Savage (D-ILL) asserted that "resource exploitation" was the reason behind the war with the United States and other developed countries behind making their own market of soon to be vanquished country's resources. Explaining, "resource exploitation he clarifies" . . . where nations exploit the resources of underdeveloped nations so that the underdeveloped nations suffer increasing poverty . . . while the developed nations with the Eurocentric culture, the capitalist economy, prosper."[44]

Ronald Dellums, Chair of the CBC, used passionate pacifist language to reshape his situational previous rhetorical support of the AVF and African Americans in military service to frame his newly found opposition to the war. He accused the Bush administration, the Senate, and the House of Representatives of cavalierly holding the lives of young men in their hands for the purpose of advancing war. He also decried that war was a venture for those who wanted to engage in killing other human beings, simply for the wanton annihilation of them. "Only a madman would want to go to war . . . because war is killing death and destruction."[45] "Dellums went one step beyond his spoken pacifist opposition, taking the initiative to file a lawsuit. He and fifty-two members of the House and one member of the U.S. Senate took President Bush to Federal Court. (Dellums vs. Bush 753 F Supp 1141

D.C. Cir 1990) in an attempt to block President Bush from exercising his presidential authority to call for a buildup for a military action without a formal declaration of war before discussing it with Congress. Under Dellums' lead, the CBC supported the unsuccessful lawsuit. On January 12, 1991, almost all of the CBC voted against House Joint Resolution #77, the bill authorizing the use of force against Iraq. The sole Republican member Gary Franks (R-Conn) of the CBC voted for it. Meryn Dymally (D-CA) was not present to vote but indicated he would have voted no had he'd been there.[46]

Once the war started, some CBC members joined African American civil rights leaders, clergy, and antiwar protestors to fight against the war. Jacquelin Howard Matthews noted that

> . . . surprisingly to some observers, a decisive number of black congressional members did not succumb to the notion "when at war, loyalty to the flag." The oppositional consistency of African American representatives in the Congress and the waning of their colleagues critical attacks against the policy is instructive. Although the majority of blacks in Congress are active in the Democratic Party and loyal to the party line, many of them participated in antiwar rallies. They became some of the most outspoken critics of U.S. policy even after the House of Representatives (215 to 183) and the Senate (52 to 47) voted in favor of White House policy. Included among these outspoken members of Congress were Ron Dellums, California, John Lewis Georgia, Charles Rangel, New York, John Conyers Michigan and Cardiss Collins (Illinois) [47]

As African American leaders debated the policies regarding the Gulf War and the large numbers of black troops deployed, other leaders who happened to be African Americans found the universal rhetorical situational language used by black leaders in Congress, churches, civil rights organizations, and the black media to describe their service less than wanting. The *Amsterdam News* claimed that there was a "war plan to re-whiten America by luring more and more Eastern Europeans to these shores thereby reducing employment opportunities for Black Americans."[48] Comments like this no doubt were on former Secretary of State Condoleezza Rice's mind when she spoke to African American journalists at the 1991 National Association of Black Journalist Convention and expressed her dismay about the black media coverage of African Americans in the war, deeming it negative and counterproductive:

> When I listened to some of the commentary about African American soldiers in the Persian Gulf, my heart really ached because the notion that somehow those poor kids were just not bright enough to know what they were getting themselves into, I think was a quite pernicious message to send.[49]

WILLING TO SERVE: MYTH OF CANNON FODDER TROOPS IN OPERATION SHIELD/DESERT STORM

The "black troops as cannon fodder" situational rhetoric used by African American leaders still remained a problem that stuck in the proverbial craw of the black service members troops who served during Operation Shield/Desert Storm. Moskos compiled pertinent data that refuted the contention of African Americans being cannon fodder in past U.S. wars and conflicts from 1975 to 1993. In Mayaguez (1975), Lebanon (1983), Grenada (1983), Panama (1989). Gulf War, Somalia (1992–1993), five hundred Americans had been killed from 1975–1993, 78 of them African American with 15.0 blacks as percentage total, slightly more than the African American population average.[50]

The other prevailing question, whether it was just poor African Americans who entered the military out of desperate economic necessity was another issue to be dealt with. President George H. W. Bush took that question on during an African American Heritage Month White House event in 1991. While speaking to national media about African American military service, he lauded the equal opportunities that the armed forces offered blacks, especially since the advent of the AVF. In his remarks, the president firmly pushed back against African American leaders eschewing the cannon fodder situational rhetoric espoused by his critics.

> To those who question the proportion of blacks in the armed forces today, my answer is simple. The military of the United States is the greatest equal opportunity employer around. . . . Every solider, sailor airman, coast guardsman and Marine have enlisted because they want to be a part of the American Armed services, because they know it is a place of openness and true meritocracy and because they know that every serviceman and woman receives equal training and the finest training and equal treatment every step of the way.[51]

Prior to the president's speech in November 1990 General Colin Powell used "the quality volunteers want to serve and they serve well" situational rhetoric to counter African American leaders' assertions that blacks would take heavy casualties in the Gulf because they are disproportionately represented.

> If one out of four, roughly one out of five is black, if the whole force accepts causalities, what would you wish me to do? Move the blacks from the positions they're in so that they will have a lower percentage of causalities? Every part of the force whether it's Hispanic Americans, Pacific Americans or lower income white solider, will probably sustain casualties in relationship to the percentage that they present in the overall force. What you keep wanting me to say is that this is disproportionate or wrong. I don't think it's disproportionately wrong. I think it is a choice the American people made when they said have a volunteer Army and allow those who want to serve to serve.[52]

Powell has traditionally used his own life story as a rhetorical situational structure to show how the military served as his upward mobility ticket. Being in the military allowed him to travel, get an education, provide for his family, and have a little adventure. He became the youngest Chairman of the Joint Chiefs of Staff at the age of fifty-three and went on to become the highest ranking African American officer in military history. Powell testified before the House and the Senate several times during the war buildup and during the war spoke about the quality of African American servicemen and women serving in the Gulf and the abilities they have to do their duties. "I'm proud of the fact that African Americans have seen fit to volunteer to join the armed force even if it is a high percentage than the general population. . . .: it annoys me when value judgements are put on it , that somehow its's bad."[53]

Elaborating on the equal opportunity of the military versus the lack of equality in the civilian corporate business sector, Powell praised the military's upward mobility challenging those in the civilian arena. "I wish corporate America, I wish the trade unions around the nation would show the same level of openness and opportunities to minorities the military has."[54]

African American Gulf War troops continued to receive support from World War II and Vietnam troops, especially Tuskegee Airmen and others. While General Benjamin O. Davis Jr. outlined in his memoirs *"American"*[55] the pride of having served his country and being a role model for Gulf War African American service members U.S. Air Force Colonel Fred Cherry, the longest serving African American Vietnam prisoner of war, also pledged his support of the Gulf troops saying he knew for a certainty that black servicemen and women of his era also supported them even though he knew that black leaders would disagree with them. Retired army Lt. Gen. Julius Becton Jr. derisively chastised African American leaders who referred to black troops in the Gulf as "mindless cannon fodder." "The problem with these people who say the soldiers especially the black soldiers are over here because they have no options is they haven't taken time to go talk with those quote dummies," Becton stated.[56]

During Operation Desert Storm, espirit de corps was at an all-time high. African American service members were glad to serve in an organization where they were treated with respect and were able to do the jobs they had volunteered to do. While racism did exist, it was for the most part far less than one would find in the civilian sector. When their Congress representative came to visit them, they were only too glad to discuss these issues.

Military members who served in the Gulf War resented the inference behind the negative connotations of cannon fodder and took it as lack of support from black leaders who appeared to be ignoring the good job they were doing and the achievements that they made during the war. Other senior military African American officers told Moskos about their frustration with black leaders, one noting, "I just tune out the so-called leadership when it comes to anything military."[57]

Those who spoke to the troops found out that they did not appreciate the characterization of the social class and their ability to serve. Moskos spent weeks in the Gulf talking to servicemen and women who in turn told him of their dismay of being portrayed as people who joined the military because they were either too poor or too stupid to do anything else.

> You can't be for the troops and demean them in the same breath. Even before the shooting started they were very aware of the antiwar movement and the image of them as a bunch of losers. They didn't like to be thought of as losers. These people who think these men and women are cannon fodder, poor misguided people with no other choices, are in a very real way condescending to the troops. That why they (U.S. military personnel) react negatively to the protest movement—they see it as putting them down.[58]

Edwin Dorn, Undersecretary of Defense for Personnel and Readiness, also dispelled the myth of just poor African Americans entering the armed forces by noting that the young people who go into the military aren't the ones who sell drugs on some Washington, D.C., street corner. "They are more likely to be highly trained and are far better than those who served in Vietnam. . . . These young black people are not from the underclass. Actually they are from the middle or working class . . . they don't think of themselves as cannon fodder or victims. They think of themselves as professional doing a job they are very well trained to do."[59]

CONCLUSION

Did African American leaders or the national black media really understand or support black troops by insisting on holding onto the Vietnam "cannon fodder rhetoric." Perhaps the question Deputy Commander of Desert Storm Lt. General Calvin Waller posed to them during Desert Storm is appropriate: What are your leaders doing in our communities to get our young black men off of drugs? What are they going to keep them in school or not dying in the streets? When the Gulf War started support among African Americans was 27 percent in early January 1991, down from 66 percent in September of 1990. Some critics believe it was because of the virulent antiwar sentiments spread by African American leaders in pulpits, antiwar rallies and marches, and African American media even in beauty and barber shops. African American combat deaths during the war were 15 percent, a lot lower than predicted. African American women served for the first time in large numbers; of the 41,000 women who served in the Gulf 40 percent of them were African American women (several were injured and three died in the conflict). Finally, African American participation in the Gulf War showed that this military conflict had won the armed forces bragging rights as an institution of opportunity for American blacks willing and proud enough to serve their country.

NOTES

1. *American Heritage from Saigon to Desert Storm: How the U.S. military reinvented itself after Vietnam*, http://www.americanheritage.com/content/saigon-desert-storm.
2. David J. Armor, "Race and Gender in the U.S. Military," *Armed Forces and Society* (0095327X) Fall 1996, volume 23, issue 1, 7–27.
3. https://www.merriam-webster.com/dictionary/cannon%20fodder 2018.
4. *American War and Military Operations Causalities: Lists and Statistics*, https://fas.org/sgp/crs/natsec/RL32492.pdf.
5. In 1975, 32 percent of African Americans lived 50 percent below the poverty line, in 1992, 49 percent lived 50 percent below it. African Americans had turned into the haves and have-nots. Increasingly African Americans joined the armed forces to escape poverty and racism and take advantage of getting a college education. Director of the NAACP Benjamin Chavis spoke of this, naming it an "involuntary draft as an economic condition."
6. Chris John, Assistant Secretary of Defense for Force Management and Personnel, argued against civil rights leaders, noting that "no one is making them enlist. They're not victims, they are willing patriotic Americans." *New York Times* January 1991 edition War in the Gulf: The troops; Blacks Wary of Their Big Role as Troops. By Isabel Wilkerson Special to the *New York Times*. http://www.nytimes.com/1991/01/25/us/war-in-the-gulf-the-troops-blacks-wary-of-their-big-role-as-troops.html?pagewanted=print.
7. Juan Williams, "Race and War in the Persian Gulf: Why are Black Leaders Trying to Divide Blacks from the American Mainstream?" *Washington Post*, January 20, 1991.
8. Lloyd Bitzer, "The Rhetorical Situation," *Philosophy and Rhetoric* 1 (January 1968). Dorothy Pennington, "The Rhetorical Condition as Mediator in the Response of African Americans to Perceptions of Terrorism: Condoleezza Rice as Symbol," *Howard Journal of Communication* 22 (2011): 123. Mellissa Renee Harris and Ashely R. Hall. "My Living Shall Not be in Vain: The Rhetorical Power of Eulogies in the Face of Civil Unrest," *Journal of Contemporary Rhetoric* 8 (2018): 3.
9. Charles Moskos and John S. Butler, *All That We Can Be: Black Leadership and Racial Integration the Army Way* (New York: Basic Books, 1996), 110, 111.
10. "The Battle for Respect," *Newsweek*, March 10, 1991, http://www.newsweek.com/battle-respect-201560.
11. David Armor, "Race and Gender in the US Military," *Armed Force & Society* 1 (Fall 1996): 7–27.
12. Ron Walters, "Why Should Blacks Fight in the Gulf?" *Washington Post*, December 27, 1990. At the time the article was written, Walters was the Chair of the Sociology Department at Howard University, District of Columbia.
13. On March 27, 1969, Secretary of Defense Melvin Laird announced the creation of the President's Commission on an All-Volunteer Armed Force. It was chaired by Thomas Gates, former secretary of defense under President Dwight D. Eisenhower; Anderson served as White House liaison. Nixon's charter was clear: the mission was not to evaluate the possibility of ending the draft, but to "develop a comprehensive plan for ending conscription and moving toward an all-volunteer forces."
14. Ibid. Military analyst Martin Binkin, Brookings Institution, 1991.
15. Gail Buckley, *American Patriots: The Story of Blacks in the Military from the Revolution to Desert Storm*, (New York: Random House, 2001).
16. Melvin R. Laird, "Equal Opportunity and Race Relations in the Department of Defense," *Commander's Digest* 12.2 (May 18, 1972): 1–2.

17. Doug Bandow Cato Institute Foreign Policy Briefing No. 6, *The Voluntary Military: Better than a Draft*, accessed from https://object.cato.org/sites/cato.org/files/pubs/pdf/fpb006.pdf.

18. Numbers attained from Gayle White, "Largest Black Church is finding Strength in Heritage," *Atlanta Journal and Constitution*, February 1991 M4.

19. Ibid.

20. Clarence Page, "Blacks Should be able to Be all they can be—as Civilians," *Chicago Tribune*, January 23, 1991.

21. The S2104 Civil Rights Bill of 1990 was introduced by Senator Edward M. Kennedy (D, Mass). It was a bill to amend the Civil Rights Bill of 1964 that was to restore and strengthen civil rights laws than ban discrimination in employment and for other purposes. George H. W. Bush felt it was quota laden. After it was vetoed it was not overridden by 2/3 majority.

22. Keynote speech given during the 110th anniversary year of the denomination. Cited in *Out of the Moral Thicket: The American Christian Religious Leaders and the Persian Gulf War*, 2001, Adelyn Fullerton, University of Purdue, 2001. Dissertation: American Studies Association.

23. Ibid., 173.

24. Lynda Richardson, "Preserving the Black Church's Bridge: Progressive National Baptist Convention leader Stresses need to Solidify Community," *Washington Post*, December 1, 1990.

25. Sam Fulwood III, "Black Activists Urge Bush to Declare Cease Fire: Dissent: Religious and Civil Rights Leaders Express Outrage over War and Threats They See to Social Problems," *Los Angeles Times*, http://articles.latimes.com./print/1191-02-16/news/mn-1046_1_civil-rights-activists.

26. Father George Clements is the founder of One Child, One Church National Adoption initative. He was the first priest assigned to Holy Angels Church in 1969. These comments came from a series of local TV and newspaper interviews. Comments found in Frank Burgos interview "Regrets over Minorities Role: Black leaders say Burdens of War Unfair," *Chicago Sun Times*, February 1991.

27. Jeanne Theoharis, "Coretta Scott King and the Civil Rights Era of the Hidden Woman," *Atlantic Magazine*, https://www.theatlantic.com/author/jeanne-theoharis/.

28. Fullerton, *Out of the Moral Thicket: The American Christian Religious Leaders and the Persian Gulf War*, University of Purdue, 2001. Dissertation: American Studies Association, 152, 2001.

29. Ibid., 157.

30. Ibid., 157.

31. Ibid., 158.

32. Juan Williams, *Washington Post*, February 7, 1991.

33. Juan Williams, "Race and War in the Persian Gulf," *Washington Post*, January 20, 1991.

34. Sam Fulwood III, "Black Activists Urge Bush to Declare Cease Fire: Dissent: Religious and Cvil Rights Leaders Express Outrage over War and Threats They See to Social Problems," *Los Angeles Times*, http://articles.latimes.com./print/1191-02-16/news/mn-1046_1_civil-rights-activists.

35. Ronald Smothers, "Now Atlanta Gets Down to Brass Tacks," *New York Times*, September 20, 1990, B1.

36. The meeting was held at the historic Harlem Abyssinian Baptist Church. "Bush's Rebuff to Iraq dismays black leaders," *The Boston Globe*, February 16, 1991.

37. Arch Puddington, "Black Leaders vs. Desert Storm," January 1991: 34, https://www.commentarymagazine.com/.

38. Rep. Waters interviewed by Lynne Duke, "Emerging Black Anti War Movement Rooted in Domestic Issues," *Washington Post*, February 8, 1991, A 27.

39. Julie Johnson, "Blacks: Too much of the Burden," *Time* 0040781X Vol 7, Issue 5, February 4, 1991.

40. Henry Richardson III, "Gulf Crisis and African Americans," *The American Journal of International Law*, (1993), 42–82.

41. Congressional record, 102nd Congress 1st Session January 11, 1991, p. H254.

42. "Race and War in the Persian Gulf," editorial (multiple authors), *Washington Post,* February 2, 1991. This article was written in response to the editorial written by Juan Williams, January 20, 1991.
43. Puddington, "Black Leaders vs. Desert Storm," *Commentary Magazine*, May 1991, https://www.commentarymagazine.com/.
44. Ibid., 29.
45. Ibid., 29.
46. Congressional Record 102 Congress 1st Session January 11, 1991 p. H254.
47. Jacquelin Howard Matthews, "African Americans and the Persian Gulf Crisis," "African Americans and the Military" *Trotter Review* 7, Issue 1, Article 10.
48. Puddington, "Black Leaders vs. Desert Storm," *Commentary Magazine*, May 1991, https://www.commentarymagazine.com/.
49. Williams, "Double Talk from War Protestors," *Washington Post*, February 1991.
50. Moskos and Butler, *All That We can Be: Black Leadership and Racial Integration the Army Way*, (New York: Basic Books, 1996)
51. Andrew Rosenthal, War in the Gulf: The Black G.I., Blacks are hailed by Bush for their Role in the military. *New York Times*, February 25, 1991. This speech was given at a White House ceremony for African American heritage month. General Colin Powell was in attendance as was Franklin Jennifer, Howard University president, and Dorothy Height, president of the National Council of Negro Women, and several members of the Tuskegee Airmen.
52. Lynne Duke, "General Powell notes Military Enlistment Remains Matter of Individual Choice." The Armed Forces have Always Provided Opportunities for Blacks. *Washington Post*, November 28, 1990.
53. Duke, "Emerging Black Anti War Movement Rooted in Domestic Issues," *Washington Post,* February 8, 1991.
54. United States Congress, House Committee on Armed Services, National Defense Authorization Act for Fiscal years 1992 and 1993-H.R. 2100 hearing 102 Congress 1st Session, Feb 7, 1991 (Washington, DC: Government Publishing Office, 1991), 76.
55. Benjamin O. Davis Jr. *American* (Washington, DC: Smithsonian Institute Press, 1991).
56. Williams, "Double Talk from War Protestors," *Washington Post*, February 7, 1991.
57. Moskos p. 113.
58. Ibid., 2.
59. Richard Cohen, "Blacks and War," *Washington Post*, January 23, 1991. This article is in response to an editorial written a week earlier by Juan Williams on Janaury 20, 1991.

Afterword

How to Place These Fine Essays into Larger Contexts

Peter Karsten

But first: The more thought I gave to this subject after having read these essays and initially conceived of my own comments, the closer I came to a kind of personal identification with the topic—call it, an epiphany. Before offering the comments indicated by this entry's title, I ask readers to first suffer me unburdening on that epiphany, as it seems consistent with some of the very ways I suggest placing these essays "into larger contexts."

I'm now convinced that, like the subject of most of those described in these essays, *my own* service experience was also instrumental in leading me to form strong antiracist views that led me to take civil-rights-oriented actions.

Growing up in Connecticut in the 1940s and 1950s, I interacted with virtually no blacks. As a golf-course caddy one summer, I noticed only one black caddy. He looked uneasy among us, though I recall no one disrespecting him. I vacationed as a pre-teen in the South with my parents, and as we drove there, I recall seeing blacks working along Route 1 in chain gangs. I then received a scholarship to a Connecticut-area prep school where my ninety classmates were all white males. The navy provided me with a scholarship to Yale, where there were, then, few blacks.

But as a midshipman and junior officer on board ships in the late 1950s and early 1960s, I saw clear incidents of racism. En route my first midshipman cruise I witnessed a black railway conductor being unduly insulted by a ridiculously irate Virginian, who appealed for support to two bewildered and shocked Connecticut-bred uniformed midshipmen!

On both midshipman cruises, and on my three-year tour of duty on a guided-missile cruiser, I saw as well how black seamen and wardroom messmen were treated by their white superiors. On my last midshipman cruise, I stood the in-port officer-of-the-deck watch one night with a black 2nd class quartermaster. I asked him whether he thought his being black had affected his treatment by superiors, and he was frank in letting me know of troubling such instances. I later overheard the ship's Southern-bred medical officer complaining bitterly to his wardroom mates of that quartermaster having refused to move to the back of the naval base's minibus. I recall making a remark defending the man, and drew an angry look from that officer.

When I left the service in August 1963 and visited my parents before heading for Wisconsin for graduate study, I watched Dr. King's famous speech at the Washington Mall on TV.[1] That prompted me to call the New Haven–area head of the NAACP and ask to join. (I still have that membership card.) I accepted an offer at the University of Pittsburgh in 1967, became involved immediately in several civil rights demonstrations, and urged voters in 1968 to vote for Dick Gregory for president on the Peace and Freedom Party (before personally deciding by late October that such a vote would be a throw-away vote helping Nixon). Thereafter I supported Democratic activist candidates uniformly, and am a Democratic committeeperson in my borough that just this year ousted an ineffective white PA legislator in favor of a young black activist woman.

In short, my service days were eye-openers for me, and in that sense I may be an example of how *some whites* were *also* drawn into the civil rights movement as a consequence of their military service.[2] Thus this subject really resonates with me, and I pleased that I've learned more about it from these essays.[3]

"AND NOW FOR SOMETHING COMPLETELY DIFFERENT!"

These essays clearly add to our insights into how and why some black veterans acted to secure civil rights for themselves and others, offering specific examples of it. Hal Friedman's Forward masterfully summarizes what has and hasn't yet been written on the impact of twentieth-century wars on the post-service role of black military personnel in the civil rights movement.[4] I hope to embellish these contributions with some additional topical-minded observations. Topical ones—because one can gain more insights in locating the accounts of these black service personnel in specific contexts: Background Characteristics; Differing Entry-level Decisions; and Differing Military Service Experiences.

Background Characteristics

Big Bill Broonzy's pre-service home in WWI was in the rural Mississippi Black Belt, where his people lived in virtual peonage and constant fear of white landlords and Klansmen. There he had little sense of racial or economic security, and chose to abandon his wife and migrate to a vibrant black world in Chicago, where he flourished professionally. He had clearly been affected by such service-related phenomenon as the cleanliness standard. "I wanted to be clean . . . [and to] be around in public places and meet people and get along with people . . . It opened my eyes. . . ."

But Kevin Greene offers little evidence of Broonzy entering into measures of a distinctly civil rights character upon Broonzy's return. In contrast, once Selika Duckworth-Lawton's black Korean War veterans returned to Bogalusa, Louisiana, they reentered a tightly-knit black community with an ideal defensive landscape, located in the vicinity of a number of military facilities. These background characteristics inspired them to organize themselves in effective armed self-defense of their families and themselves. And in this regard the Deacons of Defense and Justice also served as a successful alternative to the non-resistance methods of the mainline black civil rights movement in the South.

Harold Cruse's work[5] has explored the development of diverging paths many blacks took, beginning in the late nineteenth century. He contrasted two trajectories: An Integrationist one (NAACP, CORE, and SCLC), largely led by better-educated, often northern, frequently lighter-skinned blacks, who believed they and their race were being denied lawfully mandated and realistic access to jobs, voting, education, and housing. The other: Separatist (Booker T. Washington's fingers-of-the-hand Tuskegee plan, Marcus Garvey's UNIA, and the Nation of Islam), largely populated by less-educated, often southern, darker-skinned blacks, who doubted that whites would ever grant them rights, and sought to secure them within their own enclaves.

These diverging perspectives clearly informed the low enlistment rates of blacks in the South in WWI and WWII.[6] Thus Samuel Stouffer's Army Research Branch data found that northern and better-educated black army servicemen in WWII were over two times more willing to volunteer, as well as to serve in overseas combat units, than were their black southern and less-educated black counterparts.[7] The data also found that, during the Battle of the Bulge in December 1944, when army leadership called for black volunteers (from segregated units in the area) to volunteer to serve as replacement units for the decimated army units engaged there, those volunteers were more northern and better educated than that population's percentage among the black army population in the European Theater of Operations.

The same pre-service differences, this time between Navajos and Zunis who served in the army in WWII, led their Native American communities to react quite differently to them upon returning home.[8]

One of a large number of black veterans of WWII who testified before a congressional committee in December 1946 about the widespread denial in Mississippi of blacks to register and vote there got very specific:[9]

"We are forced to obey county and city laws, and you in turn disobey the highest court in the U.S. [the *Smith v Allright* decision in 1944 which outlawed the all-white party primary]. I say 'Is this what I fought for?'"

I can't be sure of that vet's level of education, but it seems likely his familiarity with that decision and his use of it suggests his perspective was that of an integrationist deeply committed to the advancement of civil rights for blacks.

Background characteristics may also help to explain the scandalous behavior of members of the West Virginia National Guard military police stationed at the Abu Ghraib POW facility during the war in Iraq. These soldiers were not elites, not as well-socialized by the army's norms of conduct, as expressed in the Soldier's Creed, taught during U.S. Army Basic Training and recited upon gradation:[10]

> I will never do anything, for pleasure . . . which will disgrace my uniform, my unit, or my country. I will use every means I have, even beyond the line of duty, to restrain my Army comrades from actions disgraceful to themselves and to the uniform.

Differing Entry-Level Decision-Making

Blacks soon learned that entry into the National Guard units in the era of the Vietnam War was uncommon, as these units and those of the Army Reserves were not being deployed to the war zone and served as a refuge from the war of numerous whites bent on avoiding the draft. Moreover, those blacks who had enlisted in the regular army prior to being deployed to Vietnam returned from the war with far less of a sense of alienation from the greater American polity than did those who were drafted, even when one controls from combat experiences.[11]

As Elizabeth Desnoyers-Colas makes clear, black enlistees in the era of the AVF and the Gulf War saw their service in a far more positive light than did the civil rights and black ministerial elites in the 1990s. From the 1950s on, military careers have offered blacks better financial security, and largely racist-free opportunities than were available in the civilian world. And on that note let me add to Jeremy Maxwell's insights that in 1963 Defense Secretary McNamara helped black married personnel significantly when he issued the directive that off-base housing properties in the vicinity of the many southern military bases that denied blacks leases in discriminatory fashion were to be designated as off-limits to all military personnel.

Army vet and military sociologist Charles Moskos wrote an insightful research-based essay for the *Atlantic Monthly* in 1986.[12] He offered evidence similar to what Professor Desnoyers-Colas provides in her essay. By 1986 blacks in the military occupied "more management positions . . . than . . .

business, education, journalism, government or any other significant sector of American society." Moskos quotes Black Specialist William Jones, who had grown up in a Cabrini-Green unit in Chicago, on his interaction with some of those he'd grown up with in a return to his neighborhood:

> There still hanging around waiting for something to happen. They'll never grow up. They'll always be losers. We don't have much to talk about anymore.

Moskos asked Sergeant Major Harold Smith why he remained long enough to compete successfully for promotion to what is the highest rate for enlisted personnel. Smith replied: "I wanted to teach young black solders how to make it in a white man's world. . . . You have to adapt to the Army; it's not going to adapt to you." Moscos noted the rift between civilian leaders of "the black community," and their black counterparts in the military leadership. "It galls them . . . that blacks in the military have chosen to pay their dues in the white system, not the black one; as a result, career blacks in the Army have less . . . affinity with established black organizations. . . ."

Civil rights leaders have offered less criticism of the numbers of blacks in the services since the Gulf War, but most blacks in the services continue to take pride and express satisfaction with their decisions to serve. One example is their positive attitude, compared to that of their white counterparts, in Operation Uphold Democracy, the deployment to restore the elected president of Haiti to power after he had been deposed by a military coup.[13]

Differing Military Service Experiences

Robert F. Jefferson's study of blinded WWII veterans clearly is grounded on the fact of their service-related injuries. Their trajectories, described in rich detail here, help us to understand how black and white victims of these blinding incidents resulted in their acquiring profoundly different outlooks on racial discrimination than those of their sighted military counterparts.

Blacks who entered the army as enlisted personnel quickly learned that advancement to an officer's rank was not "in the cards," at least until well into the twentieth century. The black army serviceman who wrote to the *New York Freeman* in the late winter of 1886 was probably well educated, for he addressed our collegiate friends of high mental attainments and still higher expectations, of which plethoric salaries and perspective shoulder-straps form the principal component, I would most emphatically say, my colored brother, do not come, you will never get there. . . . Since the organization of the four colored regiments now in the service, not a single colored soldier has been promoted from the ranks to the grade of officer. . . . It is not that they don't possess the necessary qualifications for the office, but that the sentiment of the white men of the army is decidedly against it, and any aspirant for shoulder-straps in the ranks is promptly & effectively given to understand that "spades are not trumps" here.[14]

For the great majority of WWII vets, their service experiences had impacts on their future earning powers that varied by race and ethnicity. The massive study of that subject drawn from the U.S. Census Bureau's 1960 Public Use Sample (1/100th) and limited to those vet and non-vet males from the five southwestern states (California, Arizona, New Mexico, Colorado, and Texas) revealed that when one controlled for level of education and type of occupation, Hispanic and (to a lesser, but still noteworthy extent) black vets were earning *more* by 1960 than their non-vet counterparts, while white vets were earning slightly *less*. The service experience appears to have prepared those from more rural, more task-oriented work environments to function effectively in order-driven, hierarchic 9-to-5 (indeed sunset to sundown), structured, environments, something a greater percentage of whites were already familiar with. It thus functioned, as they put it, as "a bridging environment."[15]

The same can be said of those Navajo personnel who served in the army in WWII. Those whose assignments required of them that they know English and be assigned responsibilities above those at low levels, took away from the service, experiences that served them well in their Rimrock Reservation community and led "John Nez" and "Yazi Begay" to regard themselves as distinct from what "Nez" called "the reservation Indian." Those who never acquired these skills simply returned to their homes, unaltered, with bewildering accounts of the "many moons" they had been away, the strange animals (camels) they encountered in the desert (of North Africa), and the bitter cold in the mountains (the Italian Apennines).[16]

Jeremy Maxwell's essay on Vietnam nicely lays out the opposition by black movements in the United States to the drafting of blacks, as well as their anger with the noncombat situations in 'Nam where some white servicemen openly displayed racist symbols. His analysis of the *Kitty Hawk* and *Constellation* incidents also serves us with case studies of differing military experiences. How? Because it's also the case that there existed few such racial tensions on military installations other than in Vietnam, or on naval vessels not deployed six straight tours of duty off Vietnam and not subject to the massive personnel turnover that occurred on the *Constellation*.

In any event, keeping in mind such variables as the three I've noted can help one understand why groups and individuals similar in one regard, may take differing paths and embrace different objectives because of their being different in other regards.

NOTES

1. I recall that Dr. King spoke at Yale in 1957, and at the conclusion of his remarks was told by a white southern student that what he had just said was "all well and good" but he wouldn't "want his sister to marry a Negro." Some of us laughed and applauded when King replied "Son, I don't want to be your brother-in-law; I just want to be your 'brother.'"
2. The only systematic study of post-service of white attitudes towards blacks that I'm aware of, that of George Lawrence & Thomas Kane, "Military Service and Racial Attitudes of White Veterans," *Armed Forces & Society* 22 (1995): 235–56, offers no support for my case, in that regard. But the trajectory I feel I took describes perfectly the post-service trajectory of one of my best friends among the junior officer corps on the *Canberra*.
3. In fact, the first PhD dissertation I signed off on at Pitt, Arthur Barbeau's, was published as *The Unknown Soldiers: Black Soldiers in World War* (Philadelphia: Temple University Press, 1974), see esp. chs. 4 and 5.
4. And his closing account of the black Navy WWII vet Jacob Lawrence's drawing, "The Builders," brought to mind the OWI wartime poster, a photo of two blue-collar workers, one black, the other, white, constructing an aircraft component, with the caption "United We Win."
5. Harold Cruse, *The Crisis of the Negro Intellectual* (New York: Morrow, 1967).
6. Peter Karsten, *Soldiers and Society: The Effects of Military Service and War on American Life* (Westport, CT: Greenwood Press, 1978), 66, 68; Karsten, "Who Volunteered for Service in World War II?" in *The Military in America from Colonial Times to the Present* (New York: Free Press, 1986), 335–37.
7. Samuel Stouffer, et al., *Studies in Social Psychology in WWII: The American Soldier*, 4 vols. (Princeton: Princeton University Press, 1949–50), II, 524.
8. John Adair and Evon Vogt, "Navajo and Zuni Veterans: A Study of Contrasting Modes of Cultural Change," *American Anthropologist* 51 (1949), 347–561.
9. Kermit Hall and Peter Karsten, *The Magic Mirror: Law in American History* (New York: Oxford University Press, 2009), 362.
10. From *The Soldier's Creed*, 2003 version.
11. James Fendrich and Michael Pearson, "Black Veterans Return," in Martin Oppenheimer, ed., *The American Military* (New Brunswick, NJ: Transaction Publishers 1971), 172, 176.
12. Charles Moskos, "Blacks in the Army: Success Story," *The Atlantic Monthly* (May 1986): 64–72.
13. Ronald Halverson and Paul Bliese, "Determinants of Soldier Support for Operation Uphold Democracy," *Armed Forces & Society* 23, no. 1, Fall 1996, 81–96.
14. *NY Freeman*, April 28, 1886. Cf. *NY Freeman*, Jan. 23, 1886.
15. Harley Browning, Sally Lopreato, and Duncan Poston, "Income & Veteran Status: Variation among Mexican Americans, Blacks and Whites," *American Sociological Review* 35 (February 1972): 74–83.
16. Evon Vogt, "Navajo Veterans," *Papers of The Peabody Museum* (Cambridge: Harvard University 1951), 158, 160–61. "John Nez" had ten years of pre-service schooling and was already somewhat proficient in English; hence he, unlike "Begay" and others Vogt interviewed possessed relevant pre-service characteristics distinguishing him as well as those of his distinctive service experiences.

Selected Bibliography

BOOKS

Anderson, Carol. *Eyes Off the Prize: The United Nations and the African American Struggle for Human Rights, 1944–1955.* New York: Cambridge University Press, 2000.

Appy, Christian G. *Working-Class War: American Combat Soldiers and Vietnam.* Chapel Hill: University of North Carolina Press, 1993.

Baldwin, Davarian L. *Chicago's New Negroes: Modernity, the Great Migration, and Black Urban Life.* Chapel Hill: University of North Carolina Press, 2007.

Baraka, Amiri. *Blues People.* New York: Random House, 1963.

Barton, Betty. *When the Disabled G.I. Comes Home.* New York: D. Appleton-Century Company, 1944.

Biondi, Martha. *To Stand and Fight: The Struggle for Civil Rights in Postwar New York City.* Cambridge, MA: Harvard University Press, 2003.

Black, Samuel W., ed. *Soul Soldiers: African Americans and the Vietnam Era.* Pittsburgh, PA: Senator John Heinz Pittsburgh Regional History Center in Association with the Smithsonian Institution, 2006.

Blackmon, Douglas A. *Slavery by Another Name: The Re-enslavement of Black Americans from the Civil War to World War II.* New York: Doubleday Books, 2008.

Bolte, Charles. *The New Veteran.* New York: Penguin Books, 1946.

Brooks, Jennifer E. *Defining the Peace: World War II Veterans, Race, and the Remaking of Southern Political Tradition.* Chapel Hill: University of North Carolina Press, 2004.

Broonzy, Big Bill. *Big Bill Blues: William Broonzy's Story as Told to Yannick Bruynoghe.* New York: De Capo Press, 1992.

Brundage, W. Fitzhugh. *Lynching in the New South: Georgia and Virginia, 1880–1930.* Urbana: University of Illinois Press, 1993.

Buckley, Gail. *American Patriots: The Story of Blacks in the Military from the Revolution to Desert Storm.* New York: Random House, 2001.

Child, Irvin L., and Marjorie Van de Water, et. al. *Psychology for the Returning Serviceman.* Washington, DC: Infantry Journal and Penguin Books, 1944.

Cleaver, Kathleen, and George Katsiaficas, eds. *Liberation, Imagination, and the Black Panther Party: A New Look at the Panthers and Their Legacy.* New York: Routledge, 2001.

Coates, John Boyd, et al. *Medical Department, United States Army: Surgery in World War II: Ophthalmology and Otolaryngology.* Washington, DC: Office of the Surgeon General, Department of the Army, 1957.

Crosby, Emilye. *Civil Rights from the Ground Up: Local Struggles, A National Movement.* Athens: University of Georgia Press, 2011.
David, Jay, and Elaine Crane, ed. *The Black Soldier: From the American Revolution to Vietnam.* New York: William & Morrow Company, 1971.
Davis Jr., Benjamin O. *American: An Autobiography.* Washington, DC: Smithsonian Institute Press, 1991.
Dittmer, John. *Local People: The Struggle for Civil Rights in Mississippi.* Urbana: University of Illinois Press, 1994.
Downey, Clifford J. *Images of Rail: Chicago and the Illinois Central Railroad.* Chicago: Arcadia Publishing, 2007.
Du Bois, W. E. B. *The Souls of Black Folk.* Chicago: A.C. McClurg & Company, 1903.
Dudziak, Mary L. *Cold War Civil Rights: Race and the Image of American Democracy.* Princeton: Princeton University Press, 2000.
Edgerton, Alanson H. *Readjustment or Revolution.* New York: McGraw-Hill, 1946.
Egerton, John. *Speak Now Against the Day: The Generation Before the Civil Rights Movement in the South.* New York: Knopf, 1994.
Fairclough, Adam. *Race and Democracy: The Civil Rights Struggle in Louisiana, 1915–1972.* Athens: University of Georgia Press, 1995.
Foner, Jack D. *Blacks and the Military in American History.* New York: Praeger, 1974.
Forman, James. *The Making of Black Revolutionaries.* New York: MacMillan, 1972.
Freeman, Gregory A. *Troubled Water: Race, Mutiny, and Bravery on the USS Kitty Hawk.* New York: Palgrave MacMillan, 2009.
Gilmore, Glenda E. *Defying Dixie: The Radical Roots of Civil Rights, 1919–1950.* New York: W. W. Norton, 2008.
Goff, Stanley, Robert Sanders, and Clark Smith. *Brothers: Black Soldiers in the Nam.* Novato, CA: Presidio Press, 1982.
Graham III, Herman. *The Brothers' Vietnam War: Black Power, Manhood, and the Military Experience.* Gainesville, FL: University Press of Florida, 2003.
Graham, Milton D., et al. *851 Blinded Veterans: A Success Story.* New York: American Foundation for the Blind, 1968.
Green, Ely. *Too Black, Too White.* Amherst: University of Massachusetts Press, 1970.
Green, Ely, and Lillian Smith. *Ely: An Autobiography.* Athens, GA: University Press of Georgia, 2004.
Grinker, Roy R., and John T. Spiegel. *Men Under Stress.* Philadelphia, PA: The Blackiston Company, 1945.
Hampton, Henry, and Steven Fayer. *Voices of Freedom: An Oral History of the Civil Rights Movement from the 1950s through the 1980s.* New York: Bantam Books, 1990.
Hill, Lance E. *The Deacons for Defense: Armed Resistance and the Civil Rights Movement.* Chapel Hill: University of North Carolina Press, 2004.
Honigsberg, Peter Ian. *Crossing Border Street-A Civil Rights Memoir.* Berkley: University of California Press, 2000.
House, Roger. *Blue Smoke: The Recorded Journey of Big Bill Broonzy.* Baton Rouge: Louisiana State University Press, 2009.
James, Winston. *Holding Aloft the Banner of Ethiopia: Caribbean Radicalism in Early Twentieth-Century America.* London: Verso, 1999.
Janken, Kenneth R. *Rayford W. Logan and the Dilemma of the African-American Intellectual.* Amherst, MA: University of Massachusetts Press, 1993.
Jones, Charles E., ed. *The Black Panther Party (Reconsidered).* Baltimore: Black Classic Press, 1998.
Jones, Patrick D. *The Selma of the North.* Cambridge, MA: Harvard University Press, 2009.
Joseph, Peniel E. *Waiting 'Til the Midnight Hour: A Narrative History of Black Power in America.* New York: Henry Holt and Company, 2006.
Joseph, Peniel E., ed. *The Black Power Movement: Rethinking the Civil Rights–Black Power Era.* New York: Routledge, 2006.
Karsten, Peter. *The Military in America: From the Colonial Period to the Present.* New York: The Free Press, 1980.

King, B. B. *Blues All Around Me: The Autobiography of B. B. King.* New York: Avon Books, 1986.
Korstad, Robert R. *Civil Rights Unionism: Tobacco Workers and the Struggle for Democracy in the Mid-Twentieth-Century South.* Chapel Hill: University of North Carolina Press, 2003.
Kotz, Nick. *Judgement Days: Lyndon Baines Johnson, Martin Luther King, Jr., and the Laws that Changed America.* New York: Mariner Books, 2005.
Krepinevich, Andrew. *The Army in Vietnam.* Baltimore, MD: Johns Hopkins University Press, 1986.
Kupper, Herbert. *Back to Life: The Emotional Readjustment of Our Veterans.* New York: L. B. Fischer, 1945.
Latty, Yvonne, and Ron Tarver, ed. *We Were There: Voices of African American Veterans, from World War II to the War in Iraq.* New York: Amistad, 2004.
Lee, Ulysses G. *United States Army in World War II. Special Studies: The Employment of Negro Troops.* Washington, DC: Office of the Chief of Military History, 1966.
Lentz-Smith, Adriane. *Freedom Struggles: African Americans and World War I.* Cambridge, MA: Harvard University Press, 2009.
Lewis, David Levering. *W. E. B. Du Bois: Biography of a Race, 1868–1919.* New York: Owl Books, 1993.
Lewis, David Levering. *W. E. B. Du Bois: The Fight for Equality and the American Century, 1919–1963.* New York: Henry Holt & Company, 2000.
Lipsitz, George. *A Life in the Struggle: Ivory Perry and the Culture of Opposition.* Philadelphia: Temple University Press, 1988.
Logan, Rayford W. *What the Negro Wants.* Chapel Hill, NC: University of North Carolina Press. 3d ed. Revised by Kenneth R. Janken. Notre Dame, IN: University of Notre Dame Press, 2001.
Lomax, Alan. *The Land Where the Blues Began.* New York: Doubleday Books, 1993.
MacPherson, Myra. *Long Time Passing: Vietnam and the Haunted Generation.* Garden City, NY: Doubleday, 1984.
Maxwell, Jeremy P. *Brotherhood in Combat: How African Americans found Equality in Korea and Vietnam.* Norman: University of Oklahoma Press, 2018.
Miyagawa, Steven. *Journey to Excellence: Development of the Military and VA Blind Rehabilitation Program in the 20th Century.* Lakeville, MN: Galde Press, 1999.
Mjagkij, Nina. *Loyalty in Time of Trial: The African American Experience during World War I* (Lanham, MD: Rowman & Littlefield Publishers, 2011.
Moskos, Charles, and John S. Butler. *All that We can Be: Black Leadership and Racial Integration the Army Way.* New York: Basic Books, 1996.
Nalty, Bernard C. *Strength for the Fight: A History of Black Americans in the Military.* New York: New Press, 1986.
O'Brien, Gail. *The Color of Law: Race, Violence, and Justice in the Post–World War II South.* Chapel Hill: University of North Carolina Press, 1999.
Parker, Christopher S. *Fighting for Democracy: Black Veterans and the Struggle against White Supremacy in the Postwar South.* Princeton: Princeton University Press, 2009.
Parks, David. *G.I. Diary.* Washington, DC: Howard University Press, 1984.
Payne, Charles. *I've Got the Light of Freedom: The Organizing Tradition and the Mississippi Freedom Struggle.* Berkeley: University of California Press, 1995.
Plummer, Brenda Gayle. *Rising Wind: Black Americans and U.S. Foreign Affairs, 1935–1960.* Chapel Hill: University of North Carolina Press, 1996.
Prados, John. *Vietnam: The History of an Unwinnable War, 1945–1975.* Lawrence: University Press of Kansas, 2009.
Pratt, George K. *Soldier to Civilian: Problems of Readjustment.* New York: McGraw-Hill Book Company, Inc., 1944.
Rangel, Charles. *And I Haven't Had a Bad Day Since: From the Streets of Harlem to the Halls of Congress.* New York: Thomas Dunne, 2007.
Riesman, Bob. *I Feel So Good: The Life and Times and Big Bill Broonzy.* Chicago: The University of Chicago Press, 2011.

Rosengarten, Theodore. *All God's Dangers: The Life of Nate Shaw.* New York: Alfred A. Knopf, 1974.

Sammons, Jeffrey T., and John H. Morrow Jr. *Harlem's Rattlers and the Great War: The Undaunted 369th Regiment and the African American Quest for Equality.* Lawrence, KS: University Press of Kansas, 2014.

Schneider, Mark R. *We Return Fighting: The Civil Rights Movement in the Jazz Age.* Boston: Northeastern University Press, 2002.

Shapiro, Herbert. *White Violence and Black Response from Reconstruction to Montgomery.* Amherst, MA: University of Massachusetts Press, 1988.

Shaw, Henry I., and Ralph W. Donnelly. *Blacks in the Marine Corps.* Washington, DC: History and Museums Division, Headquarters, U.S. Marine Corps, 1975.

Sherwood, John D. *Black Sailor, White Navy: Racial Unrest in the Fleet During the Vietnam War Era.* New York: New York University Press, 2007.

Shy, John W. *A People Numerous and Armed: Reflections on the Military Struggle for American Independence.* 2nd ed. Ann Arbor, MI: University of Michigan Press, 1990.

Slotkin, Richard. *Lost Battalions: The Great War and the Crisis of American Nationality.* New York: Henry Holt and Company, 2005.

Stouffer, Samuel., et. al. *The American Soldier. Vol. 2: Combat and Its Aftermath.* Princeton: Princeton University Press, 1949.

Strecker, Edward A., and Kenneth E. Appel. *Psychiatry in Modern Warfare.* New York: MacMillan Company, 1945.

Sullivan, Patricia. *Days of Hope: Race and Democracy in the New Deal Era.* Chapel Hill: University of North Carolina Press, 1996.

Terry, Wallace. *Bloods: An Oral History of the Vietnam War by Black Veterans.* New York: Ballantine Books, 1984.

Theoharis, Jeanne, and Komozi Woodard, eds. *Freedom North: Black Freedom Struggles Outside the South, 1940–1980.* Durham: Duke University Press, 2006.

Tyson, Timothy. *Radio Free Dixie: Robert F. Williams & The Roots of Black Power.* Chapel Hill: University of North Carolina Press, 1999.

Umoja, Akinyele O. *We Will Shoot Back: Armed Resistance in the Mississippi Freedom Movement.* New York: New York University Press, 2013.

Von Eschen, Penny M. *Race Against Empire: Black Americans and Anticolonialism, 1937–1957.* Ithaca, NY: Cornell University Press, 1997.

Waller, Willard. *The Veteran Comes Back.* New York: Dryden Press, 1944.

Wecter, Dixon. *When Johnny Comes Marching Home.* Boston, MA: Houghton Mifflin Co., 1944.

Westheider, James. *Fighting on Two Fronts: African Americans and the Vietnam War.* New York: New York University Press, 1997.

Westheider, James. *The African American Experience in Vietnam: Brothers in Arms.* New York: Rowman & Littlefield, 2008.

Whalan, Mark. *The Great War and the Culture of the New Negro.* Gainesville: University Press of Florida, 2008.

Willbanks, James H. *Vietnam War: The Essential Reference Guide.* Santa Barbara, CA: ABC-CLIO, 2013.

Williams, Chad L. *Torchbearers of Democracy: African American Soldiers in the World War I Era.* Chapel Hill: University of North Carolina Press, 2010.

Williams, Yohuru R. *In Search of the Black Panther Party.* Durham: Duke University Press, 2006.

Yost, Edna, and Lillian M. Gilbreth. *Normal Lives for the Disabled.* New York: MacMillan Company, 1944.

ARTICLES

Armor, David. "Race and Gender in the U.S Military." *Armed Forces and Society* 23, no. 1 (1996): 7–27.

Bates, Beth Thompkins. "A New Crowd Challenges the Agenda of the Old Guard in the NAACP, 1933–1941." *American Historical Review* 102 (1997): 340–77.
Blackburn, Alan R. "Rehabilitation of the Newly Blinded." *Journal of Clinical Psychology* 2, no. 2 (1946): 140–45.
Boyle, Kevin. "Labor, the Left, and the Long Civil Rights Movement." *Social History* 30, no. 3 (2005): 366–72.
Bradford, Caroline. "Army Rehabilitation at Old Farms Convalescent Hospital." *Military Medicine* 182 (2017): 1454–1455.
Chambers II, John Whiteclay. "The New Military History: Myth and Reality." *The Journal of Military History* 55 (1991): 395–406.
Citino, Robert M. "Military Histories Old and New: A Reintroduction," *The American Historical Review* 112:4 (October 2007), 1070–90
Coffman, Edward M. "The New American Military History." *Military Affairs: The Journal of Military History* (1984): 1–5.
Du Bois, W. E. B. "Returning Soldiers." *The Crisis* 18 (1919): 13.
Du Bois, W. E. B. "An Essay Toward a History of Black Men in the Great War." *Crisis* 18 (1919): 72.
Ellis, Mark. "'Closing Ranks' and 'Seeking Honors': W. E. B. Du Bois in World War I." *Journal of American History* 79 (1992): 96–124.
Ellis, Mark. "W. E. B. Du Bois and the Formation of Black Opinion in World War I: A Commentary on 'The Damnable Dilemma.'" *Journal of American History* 81 (1995): 1584–90.
Fenn, Elizabeth. "Beyond Jeffrey Amherst: Biological Warfare in Eighteenth-Century North America." *Journal of American History* 86 (2000): 1552–80.
Franklin, John Hope. "Rayford Whittingham Logan (1897–1982)." *Hispanic American Historical Review* 63 (1983): 596–97.
Gerber, David. "In Search of Al Schmid: War Hero, Blinded Veteran, Everyman." In *The Body and Physical Difference: Discourses of Disability*, ed. David T. Mitchell and Sharon L. Synder, 111–33. Ann Arbor, MI: University of Michigan Press, 1997.
Gittinger, Ted, and Allen Fisher. "LBJ Champions the Civil Rights Act of 1964." *Prologue Magazine* 36, no. 2 (1964): 10.
Grimsley, Mark. "In Not So Dubious Battle: The Motivations of American Civil War Soldiers." *The Journal of Military History* 62 (1998): 175–88.
Hall, Jacquelyn Dowd. "The Long Civil Rights Movement and the Political Uses of the Past." *Journal of American History* 91, no. 4 (2005): 1233–63.
Henderson III, Henry J. "The Gulf Crisis and African-American Interests Under International Law." *The American Journal of International Law* 87, no. 1 (1993): 42–82.
Hine, Darlene Clark. "Black Professionals and Race Consciousness: Origins of the Civil Rights Movement, 1890–1950." *Journal of American History* 89, no. 4 (2003): 1279–94.
Jefferson, Robert F. "Enabled Courage: Race, Disability, and Black World War II Veterans in Postwar America." *The Historian* 65, no. 5 (2003): 1102–24.
Jordan, William. "'The Damnable Dilemma': African-American Accommodation and Protest during World War I." *Journal of American History* 81 (1995): 1562–83.
Joseph, Peniel E. "Black Liberation without Apology: Reconceptualizing the Black Power Movement." *Black Scholar* 31 (2001): 2–19.
Karsten, Peter. "The 'New' American Military History: A Map of the Territory Explored and Unexplored." *American Quarterly* 36, no. 3 (1984): 389–418.
Keene, Jennifer D. "W. E. B. Du Bois and the Wounded World: Seeking Meaning in the First World War for African Americans." *Peace & Change* 26 (2001): 135–52.
Kohn, Richard H. "The Social History of the American Soldier: A Review and Prospectus for Research." *American Historical Review* 86, no. 3 (1981): 553–67.
Korstad, Robert, and Nelson Lichtenstein. "Opportunities Found and Lost: Labor, Radicals, and the Early Civil Rights Movement." *Journal of American History* 75 (1988): 786–811.
Lee, Wayne E. "Early American Ways of War: A New Reconnaissance, 1600–1815." *The Historical Journal* 44, no. 1 (2001): 269–89.
Lomax, Alan. "I Got the Blues." *Common Ground* 8, no. 4 (1948): 38–52.

Lynn, John A. "The Embattled Future of Academic Military History." *The Journal of Military History* 61 (1997): 777–89.

Murray, Paul T. "Blacks and the Draft: A History of Institutional Racism." *Journal of Black Studies*, 2, no. 1 (1971): 69.

Nisbet, Robert A. "The Coming Problem of Assimilation." *American Journal of Sociology* 50, no. 4 (1945): 261–70.

Reich, Steven A. "Soldiers of Democracy: Black Texans and the Fight for Citizenship, 1917–1921." *Journal of American History* 82, no. 4 (1996): 1478–1504.

Welsh, Richard L. "Inventing Orientation and Mobility Techniques and Teaching Methods: A Conversation with Russell Williams." *RE:view* 37, no. 1 (2005): 2–16.

Index

African American: clergy, 83; and Desert Shield and Desert Storm, xx, 81–82, 82, 86–88, 99–100; Korean War and, xix, 51–54; political leadership, xviii, 41–86, 94–97; responses to military racism, 74–77; responses to selective service, 69–71; and Vietnam, xix–xx, 64, 69–73; views of the military held by, 65, 70–72, 86–89, 98–100; and World War I, xvi, xviii, 4–8; World War II and, xviii–xix, 25
Ali, Muhammad,. *See also* Cassius Clay 71–72
All Volunteer Force (AVF), 83, 84–86
American Soldier, The , 24
Armed Resistance: and the idea of armed self-defense, 44–46; during World War II and Korean War, 51–54

Baltimore Afro-American: response to the return of black disabled World War II veterans, 21, 28–29
Black Panther Party, 71
Black Power, 46, 71
Blinded Veterans Association (BVA): creation of, 33–35
Bogalusa, Louisiana, 41, 48–49, 56; voters league of, 48–50
Broonzy, William "Big Bill," xviii; blues artistry of, 14; experiences in World War I, 1, 4; on leaving Arkansas for Chicago, 10–11; life in Arkansas, 3, 4; life in the camps of France, 6–8; on returning home after World War I, 9–10
Bush, George H. W., 81; veto of the Civil Rights Bill, 92; views regarding the All-Volunteer Force, 98

Cam Ranh Bay, Vietnam, 74, 75
Camp Lejeune, North Carolina, 75
"Cannon Fodder," controversy of, 82, 83–84, 98
Chicago Defender: reactions to the postwar return of black World War veterans, 8
Civil Rights, xvii, 35, 41–42, 58–59, 63–64, 65–66; and the Persian Gulf War, 86–89; and Vietnam, 66–68
Civil Rights of 1964, 67
Clay, Cassius, 72
Congressional Black Caucus (CBC), 94–97
Congress of Racial Equality (CORE), 42; activities in Bogalusa, 49; summer projects of, 43–44; voter education program (VEP) created by, 42–43
Constellation, riot on, 76, 77

Deacons for Defense and Justice (DDJ), xix, 41, 45; army training of, 50–53; and Black Power, 45–47; ideas of manhood held by, 57–59; in Korean War, xix; members of, 44; operational

secrecy of, 55; perceptions of, 44, 47, 54–55; protection of CORE members, 48; republicanism of, 47–48
Dellums, Ronald, 96–97
desegregation, 65–66
Desert Shield/Desert Storm, 81, 99–100
Du Bois, William Edward Burghardt, 3

"Facial Vision," 32–33; criticism of, 33. *See also* Jacob Levine

Gender: notions of manhood, 57–58
Green, Elijah "Ely": postwar activities of, 13–14; stevedoring experiences in the Services of Supply, 5

Hale, Vasco: activities with the BVA, 34; on arrival at Old Farms Convalescent Hospital, 30; service in the army, 26; wartime injuries of and reactions to disability, 26–27
Hope, James W.: and perceptions of race and blindness, 22–23

integration. *See* desegregation

Jackson, Jesse L., 91; response to the Gulf War, 91–93
Jasper, John: and reporting on Old Farms Convalescent Hospital, 21–22
Johnson, Lyndon Baines: and civil rights, 66–68; The Great Society programs of, 67, 68; and Vietnam War, 68–69, 73

Kendrick, Baynard, 22, 35. *See also Lights Out*
Kennedy, John Fitzgerald: civil rights initiatives of, 65–66
King, Coretta Scott: antiwar activities of, 89–91
King, Martin Luther, Jr.: the assassination of, 73; and Lyndon Baines Johnson, 67–68; and Vietnam, 72
King, Martin Luther III, 91
Kirby, Hilliard: reactions to blindness, 21, 22, 35
Kitty Hawk, riot on, 76–77
Korean War: army training of African American veterans during, 51–54

Ku Klux Klan (OK-KKK), 41–42; racist activities in Bogalusa, 48–49

Lang, Archie Samuel, 22; training instruction given by, 31–32
Lawrence, Jacob: artwork of, xx
Levine, Jacob: orientation strategies developed by, 32–33
Lights Out, 22, 35; responses of blinded veterans to, 35
Logan, Rayford Whittingham, xv; in 372nd Infantry Regiment, 5; battles with army racism, xvi; and New Negro ideology, 13; and Pan-Africanism, 13; service in World War I, xvi; *What the Negro Wants*, xv; World War II, xvi
Lowery, Joseph, 93–94

Meuse-Argonne Offensive: alleged failure of African American officers in, 6; participation of African American soldiers in, 6
migration: of African Americans, 11; and Bronzeville, 12; and New Negro Movement, 12
Moskos, Charles, 82

National Association for the Advancement of Colored People (NAACP): and Vasco Hale, 34
New Negro Movement: in African American history and culture, 9–10; and Chicago Blues Musicians in, 12; The imagery of African American veterans in, 9
Newsweek, 83
Ninety-second Division, 6
Nixon, Richard M., 84
Non-Violent Direct Action: and armed resistance, 44–45

Obama, Barack, 89
Old Farms Convalescent Hospital, xviii, 22–23; the closing and commemoration of, 36; rehabilitation and orientation programs at, 30–34

Persian Gulf Wars, xx
Powell, Colin, 83, 98–99

President's Committee on Equal Employment Opportunity, (or Gesell Committee), 65

racism, 2, 4–7, 24–25, 35, 48–50, 58, 69–73, 74–77, 86–89
Rander, Donald, 64

Servicemen's Readjustment Act, also known as the GI Bill of Rights, 22, 28
Services of Supply (SOS), 6
Student Non-Violent Coordinating Committee (SNCC), 42, 43; protests against selective service, 71

Terry, Wallace, 63–64

Valley Forge General Hospital, 22–23
Vietnam War, xvi, 63–64, 72–73; veterans of, 64

Voting Rights Act of 1965, 67–68

Waters, Maxine, 94–95
Williams, Russell: reflections on Old Farms Convalescent Hospital, 30, 36; rehabilitation experiences, 26; service in the army, 26
Woodard, Isaac, 35; The celebrated civil rights case of, 35
World War I, xvi, 2; American Expeditionary Forces (AEF), 2; in New Negro Movement, 9–10; Resistance to white supremacy, 8–10
World War II, 25; wounded soldiers in, 25; veterans of, 22–24, 26–28, 29–35

Young, AZ: reasons for forming the Deacons for Defense and Justice, 42

About the Contributors

Elizabeth F. Desnoyers-Colas is an associate professor of communication and Africana Studies at Georgia Southern University Armstrong Campus, Savannah, Georgia. She is the author of *Marching as to War: Personal Narratives of African American Women's Gulf War Experiences* (University Press of America, Rowman & Littlefield Publishing Group, 2014) an oral history that highlights the lives of thirteen African American servicewomen who represent various facets of professional, sociological, and interpersonal experiences typified by black women during their service in the Gulf Wars. Academe is Elizabeth Desnoyers-Colas's second career. She spent fifteen years in military service as an Air Force Public Affairs Officer (PAO) and was awarded the Defense Meritorious Service Medal upon her retirement from active duty. Her military duties included time serving as a speechwriter for senior DOD military and civilian officials on EEO/EEO related issues, operating as the Director of the Joint Task Force Information Bureau for the Haitian Refuge Humanitarian Rescue Effort and Guantanamo Bay, Cuba. She also served in Operation Desert Storm and was deployed to Central Air Forces, Forward, Dhahran, Saudi Arabia, as the Director of Public Affairs/Protocol.

Selika Ducksworth-Lawton is currently a professor of history at University of Wisconsin-Eau Claire. She earned her PhD in 1994 from Ohio State University in twentieth-century military and African American History. She researches the intersection of race, national security, civil rights, and protest. Her book, *Honorable Men: Armed Self Defense and the Deacons for Defense and Justice*, is under contract with University Press of Mississippi and is expected in press early next year. Dr. Ducksworth-Lawton is the co-author of *Minority and Gender Differences in Officer Career Progression*.

Hal M. Friedman is associate chair of history and professor of modern history in the History Program of the Department of Social Sciences, part of the School of Liberal Arts at Henry Ford College in Dearborn, Michigan. He received a PhD in History from Michigan State University in 1995. He has published a trilogy on U.S. national security policy in the immediate postwar Pacific and has recently completed another trilogy on the transition of the U.S. Naval War College from the Pacific War to the Cold War in the Pacific in the same time period. He is now working on another trilogy about American naval planning for the defense and administration of the immediate postwar Pacific. He is also a Graduate Senior Instructor in Norwich University's online Master of Arts in History Program, an adjunct lecturer of Strategy and Policy in the U.S. Naval War College's Non-Resident Fleet Seminar Program, and both the Recording Secretary and the Midwest Regional Coordinator for the Society for Military History.

Kevin D. Greene is Nina Bell Suggs Assistant Professor of History at the University of Southern Mississippi, where he is also the Director of the Center for Oral History and Cultural Heritage. He is the author of *The Invention and Reinvention of Big Bill Broonzy* (2018). Currently, he is the principal investigator for the Mississippi Oral History Project, a research initiative funded annually by the Mississippi state legislature to document the collective memory of Mississippi's culture, heritage, and institutions in the twentieth and twenty-first centuries. At Southern Miss, he teaches courses in American history, African American history, world history, research methodology, oral history, and music history.

Robert F. Jefferson Jr. is associate professor of history at the University of New Mexico. Jefferson holds a PhD in American History from the University of Michigan. He specializes in Twentieth Century United States History, African American History, Disability Studies, and Social History. He is the author of *Fighting for Hope: African Americans and the Ninety-third Infantry Division in World War II and Postwar America* (2008) and *Brothers in Valor: The Battlefield Stories of the 89 African Americans Awarded the Medal of Honor* (2018).

Peter Karsten is emeritus professor of history at the University of Pittsburgh. He is author of the prize-winning *The Naval Aristocracy: The Golden Age of Annapolis and the Emergence of Modern American Navalism* (1972), *Law, Soldiers and Combat* (1978), *Military Threats* (1984), *Heart versus Head: Judge-Made Law in 19th Century America* (University of North Carolina Press, 1997), the prize-winning *Between Law and Custom: 'High' and 'Low' Legal Cultures in the Lands of the British Diaspora, 1600–1900*

(2003), *The Magic Mirror: Law in American History* (2nd ed., 2009), was editor-in-chief of the prize-winning *Encyclopedia of War and American Society* (3 vols., 2008), the author of over forty articles and chapters, and the editor of numerous other volumes addressing military-related topics. Karsten was a Senior Research Fellow at the Hudson Institute, held visiting chairs at University College Dublin, Augsburg *Universitat*, and The Citadel, and held joint appointments at Pitt in sociology and the Graduate School of Public & International Affairs. He enjoys keeping his hand in with his research fields, golf, scuba, poker, his Democratic committee duties, and a good laugh.

Jeremy Maxwell is currently the POW/MIA Postdoctoral Fellow in the Dal Center for the Study of War & Society at the University of Southern Mississippi. There, he teaches in the History Department and performs research in conjunction with the Defense POW/MIA Accounting Agency to locate unaccounted-for service personnel from WWII forward. While predominately a historian of the twentieth-century United States, his research to date has been concerned with the African American experience in the military, the influence of key high-ranking military officials with respect to integration, the Montford Point Marines, and civil-military relations in U.S. History. His first book, *Brotherhood in Combat: How African Americans Found Equality in Korean and Vietnam*, explored the prevalence of racial tension in rear versus combat units during the period of integration.

www.ingramcontent.com/pod-product-compliance
Lightning Source LLC
Chambersburg PA
CBHW020126010526
44115CB00008B/996